Inna di Dancehall

Inna di Dancehall

*Popular Culture and the
Politics of Identity in Jamaica*

Donna P. Hope

University of the West Indies Press
Jamaica • Barbados • Trinidad and Tobago

University of the West Indies Press
1A Aqueduct Flats   Mona
Kingston 7   Jamaica
www.uwipress.com

10 09 08 07 06   5 4 3 2 1

CATALOGUING IN PUBLICATION DATA

Hope, Donna Patricia.
Inna di dancehall: popular culture and the politics of identity in
Jamaica / Donna Patricia Hope
p. cm.
Based on the author's MPhil thesis presented at the University
of the West Indies, Mona, Jamaica.

Includes bibliographical references.

ISBN: 976-640-168-3

1. Music and dance – Jamaica – History. 2. Reggae music – Jamaica.
3. Popular culture – Jamaica. 4. Dance halls – Social aspects – Jamaica.
5. Popular music – Jamaica. 6. Women dancers – Sexual behaviour –
Jamaica. 7. Violence – Jamaica. 8. Identity (Psychology). I. Title.

ML3486.J3H66 2006   781.646

Book and cover design by Robert Harris.
roberth@cwjamaica.com
Set in Sabon 10.5/14.5 x 24
Printed in Canada.

This is for my son, Bertland,
and Mama
(Edith Henry, July 1928–August 2002)

Rivers alone know.

Contents

List of Illustrations / *viii*

Preface / *ix*

Acknowledgements / *xiv*

Introduction / *xviii*

1 Setting the Dancehall Stage: The Historical Moment / *1*

2 Defining the Dancehall / *25*

3 "Love Punaany Bad": Sexuality and Gender in the Dancehall / *36*

4 "Bigging Up Dons and Shottas": Violence in the Dancehall / *86*

5 Identity Politics inna the Belly of the Dancehall / *122*

Notes / *131*

Bibliography / *146*

Index / *162*

Illustrations

1. Yellowman at his best, December 1983 / *12*

2. Sanchez, Flourgon and Daddy Lizard, Reggae Sunsplash 1989 / *13*

3. Wayne "Sleng Teng" Smith / *15*

4. A "tapeman" showcases his wares / *17*

5. The late master dancer and hype producer, Bogle (Gerald Levy) / *30*

6. Buju Banton, Reggae Sunsplash 1999 / *43*

7. Sandra Lee at La Roose / *64*

8. A contestant at Cactus Nightclub / *72*

9. Macka Diamond with Lady Saw / *78*

10. Tiger, Reggae Sunsplash 1989 / *99*

11. Ninja Man, Reggae Sunsplash 1993 / *100*

12. Scene from Sting 1991 / *112*

13. Charlie Chaplin with Ninjaman and Shabba Ranks / *119*

14. Women in dancehall regalia at Bogle's funeral / *127*

15. Dancers at Passa Passa Wednesdays / *128*

Preface

WHEN I WAS nine years old I wrote my first poem, titled "In the Market". It was a class assignment for my grade five teacher at primary school. The following morning at devotion, my principal read my poem over the public address system to the entire school. The response was overwhelming and it scared me. I felt exposed and pressured. And based on the mixed responses I realized that there were some who felt that all this attention meant I was a show-off. So, I adopted a kind of false modesty and hid my writings. This book comes at the end of a long process, during which I have finally overcome this fear. My writing is a gift and it must be shared. There is no need for false modesty.

I am a black Jamaican woman from the rural working class in the parish of St Catherine and I am a dancehall researcher. This book on Jamaican dancehall culture reflects my own journey through my precarious teenage years and my growing awareness of my ascribed position in Jamaican society. It also reflects my struggles to change my class of origin and to claim an identity that reflects these struggles. Somewhere in the middle of this project, I began to realize that my journey through dancehall culture, first as a fan and then as a researcher and student of popular culture, is a critical part of my own process of self-awareness and personal achievement. Now that I am this far down the road, I can look back and admit that my burning desire to understand the dancehall and to place it in its historical context arose from my journey through both the dancehall and Jamaican society in the 1980s and 1990s.

Although the formal research that forms the basis of this book was conducted between 1998 and 2000, my real work in the dancehall began over twenty years ago, in 1980. I became a child of the dancehall by listening to the sounds of King Yellowman on the stereo systems in various minibuses as I travelled to and from high school between Linstead and Spanish Town in St Catherine, Jamaica. I became a dancehall fan as a young adult, listening to the pulsing, heavy bass rhythms of Stone Love, Roadstar, Metro Media and Pieces that played every weekend at Club Jamaica, Tropicana or elsewhere in my hometown, Linstead, and its environs. Somewhere between my annual pilgrimage to Montego Bay for multiple stagings of Reggae Sunsplash and my descent into "almshouse" behaviour at Border Clash 1990 and Sting 1991, I earned my stripes as a hardcore dancehall fan.

In 1997, after completing my BA, I decided to research the dancehall for my MPhil thesis in the Department of Government at the University of the West Indies, Mona, Jamaica. My own immersion in dancehall music and culture, and my day-to-day interactions with Jamaicans from different socioeconomic backgrounds, had me fully convinced that there was a great deal more to this sphere than mere "vulgar" slack lyrics. The original study was carefully planned as a political science analysis of the anti-hegemonic factors in dancehall culture. But as the empirical research gained momentum, the study took on a life of its own. I was flung into the body of the dancehall. I became the pawn of the research, the conduit. My forays down the highways and byways of Jamaican dancehall culture enlightened me profoundly. I became aware that dancehall culture could not be contained in vague, imported social science theories because it was a living, breathing, organic part of Jamaican life. I followed where the research beckoned. My life was divided between my academic studies and teaching duties in the Department of Government and the insistent clamourings of the dancehall. I spent countless hours hanging out at locations where dancehall culture created a vibrant background and foundation for the "livity" and interaction of the people who patronized these places. These included hair salons, cosmetology shops, videographer haunts, nightclubs, sessions, stage shows, bars, barbershops and street corners. I managed to bridge the precarious gap between fan and researcher, although finding this middle ground was difficult. Many of my early interviewees regarded me as a middle-class, university-educated professional. In the rigid class-driven morass of Jamaican life, this perception generated responses and actions that reflected my respondents' view of their roles in opposition and deference to mine. I realized that when my interviewees adopted a "staged" identity they effectively hid the true workings of dancehall culture, and so I found myself drawing on my role as a dancehall fan. I began to wear dancehall regalia and costume, as that signified my adherence to dancehall culture. During this time, I became aware of the beauty of fat, large-breasted, big-bodied, dark-skinned women who revel in their overtly sexual displays of legs, thighs and breasts as a part of their economic and sexual freedom. From these women in both the dancehall and inner cities, I learnt to cement an already existing self-confidence into something more immanent. This incorporated a posture and facial expression that dared anyone, male or female, to make negative remarks about my style of dress – hair, jewellery, clothes or shoes. However, in conducting elite interviews, I had to tone down this provocative element, as male respondents would inevitably make sexual overtures that tampered with the interviewer–respondent relationship.

A young woman whose hair is bleached blond and who wears large amounts of silver jewellery on her arms and hands and toes and ankles may fit into the student population of the university but not so easily into its academic population. My students were delighted to have a tutor and lecturer whose style of dress paralleled theirs. They were enthusiastic and supportive of my role as a researcher in the dancehall. On the other hand, my academic standing was constantly in question, as my dancehall style of dress did not mirror the accepted physical markers and mores of a serious university academic on the Mona campus. I fought many silent and lonely battles.

Many Jamaicans outside of both the dancehall and academia were also more honest and overtly negative in responding to me as someone whose style of dress and behaviour symbolized one of those *buggu-yagga* dancehall people from "down there". These responses ranged from slight condescension to overt hostility and outright disrespect. Yet these interactions were extremely valuable, as they provided me with deep insight into the sociocultural politics of identity and self–presentation at work in Jamaica. Within and outside the dancehall, I experienced firsthand the responses that were based on symbolic readings of physical markers that characterize the lives of Jamaicans in a class-driven society.

These responses to my physical re-presentation were troubling, but I also had to deal with the problem of maintaining my sense of self and not going "native" within the inviting space of dancehall culture. I developed a necessary kind of schizophrenic personality that bordered on a kind of "sacred insanity". Here I could enter the dancehall to participate and observe in a state of almost full objectivity without being judgemental or biased. On leaving the field I could then revert to full researcher identity and debrief, document and analyse, again, in a state of near objectivity. The price of this schizophrenic activity has been high. It is now difficult for me to attend any dancehall event without automatically putting on my researcher lens. I consider the outcome, however, well worth the price.

This book comes out of my empirical research in the dancehall between August 1997 and May 2000. Where necessary, my prior and ongoing interaction as a fan of the dancehall since the 1980s has also been treated to a process of historical reinterpretation. This valuable historical experience, garnered from countless hours spent enveloped within the pulsing rhythms and in the vibrant space of dancehall culture is my most valuable tool as a dancehall researcher. It is only matched by my deep interest for and involvement in the montage of Jamaican lives from different class backgrounds and status groupings. These are the massive and crew, bungle and combulo, whose voices flit across the pages of my work on dancehall and notions of personhood in Jamaica. I continue to use my historical experience to enrich the historiography, analysis and examination of contemporary developments in dancehall culture.

The main themes of this work focus on the politics of gender, sexuality and violence as sites of identity and liberation in the dancehall. Based on my own research, I believe that these sites are key areas for the negotiation and contestation of identities within the dancehall and beyond.

It is my fervent hope that this book will contribute to the development of grounded theory on what is a contemporary process of social transformation in my own country, Jamaica. I also trust that this work will assist in formalizing conceptual tools by clarifying reliable knowledge and analyses about Jamaican dancehall culture specifically, and popular culture generally. As a child, fan, student and researcher of the dancehall, this is my only real contribution.

Donna P. Hope

Acknowledgements

THIS BOOK OWES a great deal to the input of my family, colleagues and friends. It represents the culmination of my extensive research on dance-hall culture in Jamaica towards my Master of Philosophy in the Department of Government at the University of the West Indies, Mona, Jamaica, and the extension of this research into papers, debates and discussions with my peers and colleagues. I remain deeply indebted to the Department of Government and the School of Graduate Studies and Research at the University of the West Indies for granting me the MPhil scholarship in 1997 and several research grants toward the original research for my dissertation.

I also owe a special debt of gratitude to my friend and mentor, Professor Rupert Lewis, for believing in and supporting my work from the start. Sir Lewis's unreserved encouragement and unstinting moral, emotional and academic support have been critical to the development of my academic career and the maintenance of my personal life throughout this journey.

Hume Johnson and Agostinho Pinnock have, over time, provided the invaluable resource of acting as both my frankest and harshest critics while simultaneously remaining my friends and confidantes. Without their critiques, suggestions, support and encouragement, this work would not have seen the light of day.

Special thanks to my friend and colleague Sonjah Stanley-Niaah, par-

ticularly for the encouragement, brainstorming and publication opportunities during the final phases of this work.

My close friends, in particular Floyd Morris, Carliss Nattoo-Young,
Selena Rose and Lorna Thomas, provided strong emotional support and
answered the telephone and listened during some of the most stressful
and frustrating periods of this work.

I also want to register my massive and jumbo appreciation for the
input of my colleagues Christopher Charles at City University of New
York, and Christine Cummings and Clinton Hutton in the Department
of Government at the University of the West Indies, Mona. Large up
every time!

This work has benefited significantly from the kind comments, moti-
vational words, acts of kindness and keen questions of Professor
Maureen Warner-Lewis, Livingston White, Ruthlyn Johnson, Jennifer
White-Clarke, Denise Black, Daphne Clarke, Hyacinth Clarke, Charlene
Sharpe-Pryce, Suzette Brown and Tasha Manley, as well as my numerous
students in various courses in the Department of Government and at the
University of the West Indies School of Continuing Studies and the
Institute of Management Sciences between September 1997 and May
2002. Respect due, every time!

Big up and blessings to the crew inna di dancehall and all ghetto people who allowed me access to the inner workings of dancehall culture
and their lives. Nuff thanks to David Burke, DiMario McDowell, Jack
Sowah, Ninjaman, Roy Fowl, Lenny, Sandra Lee, Tashai, Angel and
Stacey. I want to shout out to my brethren Binns, Patrick, Peter and the
Barbershop Crew from Linstead for all the dancehall sessions, round
robins and cultural groundings where I honed my skills as a participant
and an observer.

I remain indebted to Angela Harvey, of the Office of Public Affairs at
the US Embassy in Jamaica, who encouraged me to apply for a Fulbright
scholarship, and the Fulbright Foundation/US Department of State for
bestowing this award on me, allowing me to pursue my PhD in the
United States. My time in Fairfax, Virginia, provided the necessary hiatus so that I could complete the major revisions for this project. Words
cannot express my sincere thanks and love for my Fairfax family and my
colleagues and friends in the Cultural Studies Department at George

Mason University who provided me with necessary emotional and academic support during the most lonely yet stimulating period of my personal and academic life. Dalton and Donna Ebanks saved me from turning back more times than they would ever know. Mabel Smith in Maryland provided a Jamaican connection and a strengthening voice in the wilderness of elsewhere, and Claudette Sterling and Pierre Davis at Fenwick Library gave me the camaraderie that can only come from true brethrens. My batchmates and friends at George Mason University, in particular Jaafar Aksikas and Lisa Rhein, kept me focused with their encouragement and big-ups. A special hail out to my cultural studies professors at George Mason University: Paul Smith, Roger Lancaster and Dina Copelman, who were extremely understanding and supportive of this foreigner in a strange place. Bless up!

My sincerest appreciation to the University of the West Indies Press, particularly Donna Muirhead, who heard my work at the Caribbean Studies Association conference in St Maarten in May 2001. Her encouragement and unrelenting efforts, coupled with the wisdom of the UWI Press director Linda Speth, spurred me on. My editor, Erin MacLeod, and the staff of the UWI Press have all contributed to the timely completion of this work.

Finally, and most importantly, I want to thank my family for their unstinting loyalty and support. Nuff nuff love, big up and large up every time to a great man: my partner, friend, confidante and co-researcher, Marlon Marquis, who came into my life in 1999 in the dancehall and has continued to teach me more about life and love than I ever dreamed possible. Ever faithful, ever sure, every time, you live in these pages. Nuff respect and everflowing love to my son, Bertland Hope, who made the transition from boyhood to manhood during this journey. Bertland has been a supportive and loyal yute during his own chaotic transition when he did not understand why he was asked to give and give so much when he thought he had so little. The completion of this work comes with its own cache of grief and loss. The original research was conducted in the comforting shadow of my mother, Edith Henry, and it was my dream that she would see the finished product. But this was not to be. Mama left me partway along the road in August 2002 and her departure has been a psychological prod that continued what she gave me from early on – the gift of words and the courage and strength to stay the course. This is her legacy.

Those whose names I have omitted number themselves among the myriad loyal friends, colleagues, students and acquaintances who have provided support, comments and criticisms throughout the conception and delivery of this work. All these persons and institutions have, in some way, left their imprint on this book. However, I claim overall responsibility for the final product.

Introduction

THIS WORK AIMS to ease the scarcity of accessible academic work on Jamaican popular culture generally and dancehall culture specifically by exploring and analysing some of the primary symbols and narratives of gender, sexuality and violence emanating from within the dancehall. It argues throughout that these symbols and narratives play a significant role in the negotiation and contestation for public space through the dancehall's re-presentation of identities that play with and against Jamaica's hegemonic structures. Its primary adherents, inner-city and working-class citizens, must negotiate these structures through their multiple roles in postcolonial Jamaica.

These symbols and narrative ideologies exist not only in the music and lyrics of the dancehall, but also in the social, economic, political and gender dynamics operating within this space. The discourses of the dancehall operate in tension with and against the conventional, hegemonic framework of "decent" traditional Jamaica. The discursive tensions and political contestations affect the sociopolitical structures and create gaps where dancehall identities clamour for space. Consequently, since its rise to prominence over two decades ago, "slack" dancehall culture has effectively infiltrated the identity spaces and hegemonic foundation of Jamaican society. It has successfully crafted a legitimate cultural space by drawing on elements that easily merge with and sometimes move beyond the boundaries of traditional Jamaican practices, identities and politics. The current dearth of accessible and relevant sociopolitical cues and role models means that actors in the dancehall are immensely attractive to young people. When this attraction is married to its accessibility and pervasiveness, it results in a cultural product that has the power to alter the sociopolitical landscape in Jamaica. Dancehall culture's identity re-presentations proffer a magic wand that many individuals from the poverty-stricken inner cities of Kingston and St Andrew use to transform and redefine the subordinate roles and identities ascribed to them by traditional Jamaican society. This makes dancehall's "bashment", "bling bling" and hype immensely powerful.

In chapter 1, there is a discussion of the historical moment that provided the birthing ground for dancehall music and culture. An overview and analysis of the economic, political, social and cultural factors that characterized this historical framework is presented. The rise of the informal sector, trends in urbanization, poverty and crime are discussed and these intervening variables are linked with the evolution and rise of dancehall music and dancehall culture. The chapter then speaks to dancehall music and its development into a framework for cultural interaction and contestation. It sets the stage for the definition and discussion of the dancehall dis/place and its key elements.

Chapter 2 defines the dancehall and explains the conceptual framework of the term dis/place. It also outlines categories or typologies of heterogeneous actors labelled *affectors* and *affectees* within dancehall culture. These categories or typologies are also representations of gendered and cultural identity groups in the dancehall dis/place that either work in concert with, or compete against, the preferred forms of gendered and cultural identities that are proffered within the hegemonic spaces of traditional Jamaica.

Chapter 3 outlines the prominent themes of gender and sexuality at work in the dancehall dis/place and attempts to explain these themes based on research. The use of sex and sexuality as route to identity creation and maintenance is investigated and focus is placed on the courting and/or conquering of the feared *punaany* in dancehall. Female sexuality and the use of erotic display is examined and the *independent ooman, matie/ey* and *skettel* are presented as configurations of female gender identity. The politics of race, class and colour are used to analyse the use of public space afforded to the lighter-skinned Carlene, the Dancehall Queen, and the darker-skinned Lady Saw, the Queen of Slackness. Based on these discussions, this work argues against and challenges notions of and arguments for an overarching sexual liberation of women in the dancehall dis/place. I also examine the explosion of anti-male homosexual narratives in the dancehall dis/place and place this strident cultural narrative against male homosexuals at the centre of patriarchal notions of manhood and masculine status. The chapter argues for the primary role of patriarchal masculinity in defining gender roles and activities in the dis/place and points to the need for further in-depth research to illuminate the cultural and gendered negotiations of masculinities in dancehall culture.

Chapter 4 examines violence as one other central theme in dancehall culture. This discussion examines violence in the wider Jamaican society and then focuses on violence as a key factor at work in the dancehall dis/place. The nexus between urban poverty and violence and the general role of violence within the dancehall are evaluated. The more specific role of the idealized *don* or the *shotta* in the dancehall dis/place is linked to a discussion of the broader configuration of these powerful identity types in Jamaican society. The event profile of Sunsplash/Sumfest and Sting are discussed, and the Clash of Borders presaged by events at Border Clash 1990 is analysed.

Chapter 5, "Inna di Dancehall Dis/Place", merges the conceptual themes that underlay the discussions in the foregoing chapters. It deals with the politics of representation and identity and presents concluding remarks on the role of dancehall culture.

Early attempts to fit this work into an overarching theoretical framework proved problematic. In an effort to allow for organic development, I draw from different theoretical approaches and experiment with an alternative methodology within a broad social science ambit. These include Caribbean studies, cultural studies, political science, sociology and gender theory, among others. I combine historical discussion with some overview of capitalism and its impact on the development of the informal sector, as well as sociopolitical hierarchies of class and identity. However, where the overall analysis is concerned, the most pragmatic theoretical approach has been one that marries existing theories to the terrain of Jamaican popular culture and patriarchal praxis. This exercise accounted for the cultural and historical specificities of Jamaican society, including the rigid class structure that dominates the country's sociopolitical landscape. Therefore, my method of data analysis engaged grounded theory where I selected the themes and allowed a theory to emerge from the data and discourse analysis. I drew on theory and praxis to conceptualize grounded theory that is relevant to Jamaican dancehall culture and its representation of the identity contestations in Jamaica.

CHAPTER 1

Setting the Dancehall Stage: The Historical Moment

The Historical Context

THIS WORK SITUATES the evolution of dancehall music and culture in a historical context that is indelibly marked by the political, economic and social transformations of Jamaica in the 1980s. The various factors at work affected the structure of production and opened a space for transformations in the popular form of music culture. These factors included (but are not limited to) the fall-out of Jamaica's experiment with structural adjustment; the rise of free market capitalism; increasing urbanization; rising political violence; a growing ideological convergence between the People's National Party (PNP) and the Jamaica Labour Party (JLP); the explosion of Jamaica's informal economy and ongoing transformations in the class/status hierarchy, particularly among the middle strata.

In 1944, the JLP won the first general election in Jamaica under universal suffrage. That same year, a stable two-party system emerged out of the personal competition between Norman Manley of the PNP and Alexander Bustamante of the JLP.[1] During the 1950s and 1960s, both political parties held similar centrist views; however, during the 1970s, the PNP, under Michael Manley, began to project a left-wing ideology, while the JLP moved to the right.[2] As head of the PNP government that

gained power in 1972, Michael Manley attempted to implement meas-
ures to redistribute the economic gains that the country had been making during the past twenty years. Manley sought to end Jamaica's
dependency on foreign companies and replace capitalism with democratic socialism. Economically, the rapid increase in OPEC oil prices in
1974 presaged the economic crisis of that period, and in March 1976
Jamaica's foreign reserves became negative.

Despite economic setbacks, the PNP was successful in gaining a second term in office in the 1976 general elections. However, after Manley's
defiant anti-imperialistic statement that "above all we are not for sale
. . . we reject any foreign imposed solutions to the present crisis we
face",[3] the PNP government reluctantly signed a two-year Standby
Agreement with the International Monetary Fund (IMF) in December
1976.[4] This agreement's conditions were currency devaluation of
between 20 and 40 per cent and a reduction in the government's deficit.
Nonetheless, the government subsequently decided to seek other alterna-
tives and deviate from the IMF conditions.[5] In January 1977, the PNP
government initiated its own non-IMF programme. It placed controls
on trade, stopped foreign debt payment for a period of eighteen months,
reduced wage growth and sought aid from sympathetic left-wing govern-
ments. Nevertheless, the structural adjustment policies of the IMF and
the World Bank heralded the end of the democratic socialist dream pioneered under the 1970s political regime of the Manley government and
a harsh initiation into the unequal workings of global capitalism for the
island began.[6] Manley's socialist dream and his ambitious policies failed
due to grandiose schemes for governmental expansion, external political
pressures caused by his socialist rhetoric and poor implementation of
the proposed programmes.

Michael Manley's PNP government was ousted by Edward Seaga's
JLP in 1980. The JLP rode into political office on the crest of a wave of
political violence that had reportedly claimed the lives of over eight hundred Jamaicans.[7] This change in state leadership was consistent with the
two-party system created and entrenched in the Jamaican constitution
and maintained by an almost consistent pattern of alternation of state
leadership every two terms since the JLP won the first general elections
in 1944.[8] This consistent pattern of alternation was coupled with the

development from the early 1960s of a vibrant patron-clientelist frame-work for the development of largesse to loyal political supporters.[9] According to Carl Stone, the core of this "system is the exchange of eco-nomic and social favors to a poor and socially fragmented population in return for support".[10] Over time, this patron-clientelist structure has underwritten the development of a political system marked by strong partisan party loyalties, garrison constituencies and political violence, particularly among the urban poor in Kingston, St Andrew and St Catherine. Here, Stone notes that the efforts by political party bosses to assert their own hegemony over local power domains are, in the main, successful in areas where "poverty, urban ghetto conditions, careful placement of party hard-core through government controlled housing schemes and tight local organizations" exist.[11] This hegemony is asserted through the convergence of these aforementioned factors, which are instrumental in establishing "a community majority of emotionally intense party militants tied to the patron-broker-client machine",[12] that is, a garrison. Writing nearly two decades later, Mark Figueroa describes a garrison community as "a political stronghold, a veritable fortress con-trolled by a political party".[13] Any significant social, political, economic or cultural development within the garrison can only take place with the tacit approval of the leadership (whether local or national) of the dom-inant party. There are twelve communities labelled as garrisons in Kingston, St Andrew and St Catherine.[14] Other historical factors, includ-ing a strong inclination for charismatic and paternalistic leadership, served to deepen the polarity between rival political factions in the soci-ety (JLP and PNP), whose supporters had much to lose or gain depend-ing on whether or not their party was in power. This was an important facet of the political structures of 1980s Jamaica.

Under structural adjustment, "the restructuring of the Jamaican econ-omy – to reduce fiscal deficits and to achieve greater competitiveness – was the harsh experience of the 1980s".[15] Indeed, under the Seaga-led government of the 1980s, Jamaica underwent similar processes. It made and broke IMF agreements just as it had under the previous PNP admin-istration. While the economy improved, actual growth was flat or very little. Economic aid from the United States provided a significant boost and averaged US$200 million from 1981 to 1984, compared to US$47 million in 1979 under the Manley-led PNP administration. The continued failure of the IMF's programme was starkly evident in the government deficit of 1983, which at 24 per cent of GDP was vastly different from the IMF's earlier prediction in 1980 of a 1 per cent surplus.[17] In real terms, Jamaica, as part of a larger Caribbean and Latin American region, underwent severe crises as part of a broader transformation by the globalization of advanced capitalism. The country sought to move from an economy that was based on import-substituting industrialization to one that depended on the lowering of tariffs, less direct state control of the internal economy and an emphasis on export-oriented industrialization. These economic transformations carried with them social and political implications and also impacted the labour force.

For Jamaica, structural adjustment meant a contraction and deterioration in the provision of other public items, including public transportation, street cleaning and maintenance, as well as road repair and maintenance. It also meant high mortgage interest rates, increasing rents, overcrowding and urban sprawl. Where basic food supplies were concerned, it meant the removal of price controls and subsidies; in the health sector it meant fee-for-service and escalating drug prices. In education, it brought over-crowding in schools, deterioration of physical facilities and declining performance.[18] Indeed, Jamaica was just as economically strapped under the Seaga-led JLP government of the early 1980s as it had been under the earlier Manley-led PNP administration.

During this period, the primacy of Kingston as the chief urban centre[19] was undermined by a focus on tourism and the creation of export-processing zones[20] in other areas of the country. Reduced state involvement in welfare and the provision of housing, coupled with deteriorating housing conditions, resulted in population movement (both rich and poor) away from Kingston. This was part of an earlier period of change where, for example, the population of Portmore, St Catherine, moved from 2,200 in 1970 to 67,000 in 1982. By 1991, this figure had expanded to 96,700[21] and by 2004 was estimated to be over 200,000. The Kingston Metropolitan Area, which now includes Jamaica's third largest city, Portmore, is one of the largest urban areas in the Caribbean. It contains over 26 per cent of the country's population. Jamaica's total urban population grew at an annual rate of 1.42 per cent between 1991 and 2001. In 2001, over half of the estimated 2.5 million Jamaican ulation (52 per cent) lived in areas classified as urban, representing a 2 per cent increase over the 1991 share.[22]

Additionally, structural adjustment policies called for deregulations in the labour market, which impacted on employment statistics. Recorded levels of unemployment moved from a total of 175,500 in October 1975 to 268,800 for the same period in 1985.[23] Unemployment rates moved from 27.9 to 25.5 per cent between 1980 and 1984 and then declined to 18.4 per cent in 1988. However, some of the later decline in unemployment rates after 1986 can be attributed to the high levels of emigration in 1987 and 1988.[24]

The cost of living in Jamaica rose dramatically between 1983 and 1989. The J$65.31 needed to feed a family of five in September 1983 (with minimum wage set at J$30.00) moved to J$141.73 by March 1988 with the minimum wage at J$52.00. By December 1989, two and a half minimum wage incomes were required to meet the minimum food budget cost of J$207.04 with minimum wages at J$40.60.[25] Estimates of poverty in the early 1990s showed that the proportion of persons below the poverty line in Jamaica increased from 26.9 per cent of the population in November 1989 to 27.9 per cent in 1990 and 38.9 per cent in 1991. This was followed by a decline to 34.2 per cent in 1992. Statistics from the Planning Institute of Jamaica showed an increase in Jamaicans below the poverty line from 32.7 per cent in 1989 to 37.7 per cent in 1992 with a decline to 28.2 per cent in 1993. Poverty in the urban centre of the Kingston Metropolitan Area increased from 10 per cent in 1989 to 19.4 per cent in 1992 and then fell slightly to 18.6 per cent in 1993.[26]

The foregoing and other factors concentrated the existing social problems of overcrowding and low standards of living, especially among the urban poor and the lower classes, and these groups remained the most vulnerable in the midst of the economic and political turmoil of 1980s Jamaica. Deterioration in the provision of quality public health, education and transportation services; contraction in employment and housing provision; increased taxes; devaluation of the Jamaican dollar and the removal of food subsidies that came with structural adjustment were accompanied by social repercussions. These tensions were mirrored in the political arena. A populist election campaign against the harsh IMF and World Bank loan conditions helped propel Manley and the PNP back into office with a landslide victory in the 1989 general elections.

Yet the increasing inability of successive PNP and JLP administrations to develop and manage effective political, economic and social strategies to underwrite the lives of the populace forced many Jamaicans to individually seek creative ways to stay afloat in the backwash. These strategies included migrating; reducing expenditure on basic food items and items deemed as "luxuries"; foregoing personal development, including secondary and tertiary education; postponing capital investment; and creating new petty trading or informal economic activities.

During the political and economic fallout of the late 1970s and 1980s, social class and status played an important role in the development of the Jamaican informal economy. According to Anita Waters, "Jamaica's class structure today reflects its history as a colonial plantation society and its beginnings of industrial development."[27] Carl Stone's analysis of the Jamaican political economy derived three main status groupings and seven class formulations as representing the class and status structures of the society.[28] These seven class groupings fit into the three status groups: capitalists and administrative classes in the upper/upper middle class; independent property owners/middle-level capitalists and labour aristocracy in the lower middle class; and own-account workers/petty capitalists, working class, and long-term or indefinitely unemployed in the lower class.[29] It should be noted, however, that despite the emphasis placed on income and wealth in the definitions given for class positioning and status by Stone, class structure in Jamaica continues to be perceived as a rigid continuum of class rankings that subsume other factors. For example, occupational and educational prestige has been and does remain important in defining one's class and status positioning; consequently, education as a means of social and economic mobility remains important for members of the rural working class and the rural poor. To this end, Stone's three status groups and seven class groupings are more usefully collapsed into a hierarchy of five class or status groupings as follows: upper, middle, lower middle, working and lower classes. The upper classes contain the large-scale property-owning capitalists and top-level technocrats, bureaucrats and politicians; the lower classes contain the chronically underemployed and unemployed, many of whom live in the inner cities.

It is therefore important to note that in Jamaica, while both race and colour may play a role in defining status and personhood, the discontinuities based on class far supersede those that may be predicated on race and colour. A residual colour and racial differentiation, however, does remain as a part of Jamaica's plantation history. Race is still correlated with class because the greater percentage of ethnic minorities (whites, Jews, and light-coloured Chinese and Lebanese) either own property or are located at the highest levels of Jamaica's class and status hierarchy in a society where more than 97 per cent of the society is Afro-Jamaican or black. The visibility of this small percentage of lighter-skinned, upper- and middle-class individuals creates race and colour tensions that often operate simultaneously with the class divisions. As a result, the greater percentage of Jamaica's very poor and chronically underemployed and unemployed is darker skinned or black. The politico-economic situation in the 1980s as well as the failure of economic and social proposals in Jamaica resulted in the increasing impoverishment of the predominantly black lower-class and urban-poor groupings in the society. It was from among these socioeconomic class groupings that the greatest percentage of a new genre of the entrepreneurial class emerged in the informal sectors of the society.

The term "informal economy" that was originally introduced by Keith Hart[30] refers to income-generating activities that are unregulated by the institutions of a society within a legal and social environment in which similar activities are regulated.[31] Undeniably, Jamaican culture has always supported informal economic activities (for example, petty trading in ground provisions) as part of a general framework of subsistence. However, the expansion of this informal trend into a viable entrepreneurial alternative was spurred by the changes in the 1980s urban labour markets under structural adjustment. Alejandro Portes and others note the simultaneous expansion in informal employment along with a contraction in formal employment and earnings.[32] Formal employment, as the sum of government, formal services, white-collar and regulated blue-collar employment, fell from 60.4 per cent in 1977 to 53.3 per cent in 1989. Informal employment, as the unregulated employment in domes-

tic service, crafts and manufacturing, street vending, services and suburban agriculture, rose from 17.4 per cent in 1977 to 26 per cent in 1989.
These new informal entrepreneurs were driven by an aggressive and creative instinct for survival at all costs and were encouraged by the opportunities that arose in the mish-mash of structural adjustment and market
capitalism whereby the strategic harnessing of the economic principles of
demand and supply translated into enormous fortunes. As a part of this
explosion in Jamaica's urban informal economy, the development of a
thriving and unregulated export and import sector by the "higglers",
later named the informal commercial importers (ICIs) in 1983, has been
one of the most visible examples. Initially, higglers were predominantly
women from rural Jamaica who engaged in small-scale trade in ground
provisions in the rural and urban markets of Jamaica. In the 1980s, however, a new form of female entrepreneurship developed where women
from urban and rural spaces initiated informal export and import activities, beginning with their visits to countries such as Curaçao, Panama,
Bermuda and so on. They used the proceeds of their trade in Jamaican
rum and similar products to purchase foreign goods for resale in
Jamaica. Many eventually gained non-immigrant visas to the United
States and here the small-scale trading activities developed into a sector
that purchased food, clothing and other goods in the United States for
resale to wholesalers, retailers and individuals. Many of these women
made individual fortunes.[33] Their overwhelming success resulted in the
Jamaican state inevitably formalizing this sector, labelling them ICIs and
levying customs duties and formalized taxes on their activities. Based on
research conducted in 1984 and 1985, Elsie Le Franc identified a high
representation of individuals who had originally been in white-collar
jobs and lower-level professions among the ICIs (28.4 per cent) and town
higglers (14.4 per cent).[34] Other sources of informal activities included
providing public transportation via the minibus and illegal "robot"
taxis; involvement in illegal drug deals; large-scale fraud; and the trade
in foreign exchange on the black market.

The intense social pressures at work in early 1980s Jamaica demanded
a catharsis, the opening of a safety valve to release the pent-up frustrations of many dispossessed Jamaicans. From within the heart of Jamaica,
popular culture responded to the vacuum that had developed in the soci-

ety. It projected a cultural music product that was indelibly marked by the political, economic and social tensions at work in the society. This was the evolution of dancehall music and culture.

Dancehall's Evolution

In his work on Jamaican creole society, Edward Kamau Brathwaite states that creolization was a cultural action or social process[35] that affected elites and masters as well as labourers and slaves. Creolization is reflected in the dichotomy of Jamaican culture and life where the predominantly lighter-skinned elite classes continue to maintain a broad cultural and social divide between high and low cultural and social practices. The pervasive cultural dichotomy that Brathwaite identifies as the result of slavery and creole society has endured and persists in contemporary postcolonial Jamaica with the "high culture" of the predominantly brown or lighter-skinned, educated, middle classes being polarized against the "low culture" of the predominantly black or darker-skinned "unwashed masses" of the inner cities of Kingston, St Andrew, St Catherine and the lower classes of Jamaica.

Consequently, there is a constant struggle between the "superior" European culture and the African culture in the negotiation of Jamaican identity.[36] European cultural values continue to be elevated while African cultural values are denigrated[37] even while guardians of African retentions maintain challenges to the colonial European cultural ethos.[38] Dancehall music and culture, as the most contemporary manifestation of what is deemed Jamaican "low culture", actively creates and re-creates symbolic manifestations of the tensions that operate in society. The play across the field of popular culture, where the dancehall, as inner-city and lower-working-class culture, works to both produce and reproduce varied and competing forms of personhood in Jamaica.

In similar fashion to the informal, entrepreneurial activities of the predominantly female ICI sector, dancehall music and culture evolved as an organic and critical response of Jamaican popular culture to the discordant call of the social, political and economic constraints of the 1980s. Like the ICI sector, the male-dominated dancehall landscape represented a development in the petty commodity sector aggressively created by poor blacks.[39] The dancehall encompassed the thrust for economic sustenance on behalf of many dispossessed Jamaicans; the creation of a voice for the voiceless; and a bid for survival and escape from the poverty-stricken lifestyles of the inner cities of Kingston and St Andrew. The music drew on a tradition of Jamaican resistance music spanning the decades of the 1960s and 1970s (mento, ska, dub, rocksteady and roots rock reggae, for example) and ending with the death of international reggae icon and superstar Bob Marley in 1981. This new genre had its roots in the sound systems of the 1950s and 1960s and the early "toast" or "talk over" style credited to Sir Coxsone Dodd. The term "dancehall", which then defined a place for the staging of dances, was the label given to this popular musical form. Dancehall music featured deejays (DJs) and singers "toasting" or singing over a popular rhythm, many creating their lyrics on the spot. However, the impact of local, regional and global forces on dancehall resulted in the creation of a shiny new genre of Jamaican popular culture that was unmistakably related to, but significantly distinguished from, its predecessor, the Rastafari-influenced reggae music.

Dancehall music and culture burst into prominence with the popularizing of the flashy albino deejay Winston "Yellowman" Foster, otherwise known as King Yellowman, who embodied the most radical and provocative facets of this cultural sphere. Yellowman's status as an albino (*dundus*) and an orphan who was raised in state institutions put him at the lowest point of Jamaica's socioeconomic hierarchy. Yet his lyrics and performance ironically belied his pariah status, as Yellowman created and disseminated his own perception of his identity as a sexy, sexual, handsome and desirable man.[40] In this instance, Yellowman's deejaying career can be related to that of King Stitt, "The Ugly One", who was the first to have deejay hits in the late 1960s. His were, however, modelled after the jive talk of American radio deejays. Stitt's ability to use his facial disfigurement to his advantage parallels Yellowman's own subsequent example of a Jamaican artiste who overturns a physical misfortune and uses it to his advantage. Indeed, Yellowman's propensity to culturally produce and perform his own aggrandized self-identity is a trend that runs the gamut of dancehall production and performance throughout the 1980s and beyond. For example, in the 1980s, Shabba Ranks (Rexton Gordon) consistently promoted himself as the sexy, desirable "Girls Dem Pet" and sex symbol; in the late 1990s Elephant Man (O'Neil Bryan) was famed for his entreaties to video cameramen and stagehands to "shine di light inna mi cute and dainty face" as a part of his hyped performance onstage. Like Yellowman, Shabba Ranks and Elephant Man were socially handicapped because they were identified as poorly educated residents of Seaview Gardens, one of Kingston's inner cities. This placed them at the lowest point on Jamaica's class hierarchy. Moreover, like Yellowman, these two men were not blessed with facial features that were initially pleasing to the eye. Yet they and others, like Ninjaman, used the dancehall to creatively and strategically overcome these perceived deficiencies in their status and appearance. A 1991 dancehall song "Ugly Man Take Over" celebrated this lineage of unattractive but highly successful deejays, including Stitt, Shabba and Ninjaman,[41] who were able to attract many beautiful women.

Another important artiste, U-Roy, "The Originator", is credited with establishing deejaying on record as a popular form in the late 1960s to early 1970s because of his then unique way of talking over the music, instead of just interjecting at critical points, as well as riding the instrumental track to its very end. U-Roy's distinct style was related to but unlike that of his predecessor, Count Machuki/Matchukie, the first man to speak over records at dances.[42] U-Roy's three hits, "Wake the Town", "Rule the Nation" and "Wear You to the Ball", recorded for Duke Reid, held the top three positions on the Jamaican music charts for twelve weeks in early 1970.[43] U-Roy's success in the early 1970s established the phenomenon of deejaying as a Jamaican music form, but Yellowman propelled dancehall music to the forefront of Jamaica's music industry.

Yellowman's consummate skill and prowess as a deejay was cemented in his lyrics and performance that encoded the day-to-day facets of inner-city life using humour and the unsophisticated and highly sexual language that stripped away the double entendre used in earlier forms of Jamaican music. His proliferation of sexual, humourous and slack lyrics included such hits as the witty and pertinent "Soldier Take Over", "I'm Getting Married", "Belly Move" and "Zunguzungguzungzeng". Yellowman's success heralded the rise of this new genre of Jamaican music. His

Yellowman at his best, December 1983. Courtesy of the Gleaner Company Limited.

famous pornographic, slack toasts, including hits such as "Cocky Did a Hurt Me" and "Wreck a Pum Pum", were filled with lyrical toasts to and about women, sex and money, and the relationship between them. These tunes were read by some critics as indicators of "the rise of a new era of cultural artistes who stopped dealing with controversial political issues".[44] Many of these lyrics reflected the lives, realities and aspirations of the deejays and singers, and, by extension, their peers in Jamaica.

The development of dancehall and its radical deejay style did not mean the erasure of singers as a part of Jamaica's popular culture arena. In fact, singers like Beres Hammond, Gregory Isaacs, Marcia Griffiths, Dennis Brown, Cynthia Schloss and Sanchez formed an important core of the type of popular music that was played at many dancehall events. However, as dancehall music evolved, it was the deejay who became king, not the singer. Yellowman heralded this trend and paved the way for his successors throughout the 1980s, 1990s and into the twenty-first century. As with their Rastafari-influenced predecessors, these cultural artistes were, in the main, men who were products of a poor and ghetto lifestyle. Only a few came from lower-class, middle-class or rural households, and few had received any significant education beyond the sec-

Sanchez (centre) *and his then sidekicks Flourgon* (left) *and Daddy Lizard* (right) *performing at Dancehall Night, Reggae Sunspalsh 1989. Courtesy of the Gleaner Company Limited.*

ondary level. Consequently, the era succeeding Bob Marley's death reverberated with the voices of a new strain of griots from Kingston and St Andrew's inner cities. This appropriation of the power to name and call into being using dynamic and transient inner-city slang grounded in Jamaican patois signalled new powers of representation similar to those appropriated by Rastafari in the foregoing era. However, unlike their Rastafari-influenced predecessors, whose reggae songs spoke predominantly of love, peace, race consciousness, black pride, and a cultural and social revolution, the griots of the dancehall disseminated their lyrics in hard, "vulgar" dancehall and inner-city slang. They spoke chiefly to the local debates about life in the inner cities and its attendant poverty and deprivation, political violence, gun violence, police brutality, sex and sexuality, and other domestic factors that characterized life for Kingston's urban poor. There is no clear evidence that the music deliberately sought to ignore the Marley-type refrain of black pride, race consciousness and social commentary. However, it is arguable that those who rose to prominence in dancehall in the 1980s exhibited no clear attachment to the ideals and ideology of Rastafari and African pride, because the ideology of capitalism encapsulated its own ideals – individualism, materialism and its attendant moral values. My argument here in no way discounts the later emergence of Rastafari-influenced artistes such as Capleton, Sizzla and Anthony B within the dancehall genre. While these and other artistes who represent what I consider to be a hybrid "dancehall Rasta" may be mentioned herein, this group is not extensively discussed or analysed in this work.[45] In my estimation, based on the unique configuration of this hybrid, dancehall Rasta, the group deserves extensive treatment in a single work.

Advances in computer technology spurred the proliferation of dancehall music's unique toast and talk-over style when the production of the music was complemented by the development of computer-based digital rhythms. This was marked by the creation of the popular, digital Sleng Teng rhythm in 1985. Sleng Teng, seen as a watershed in dancehall history, represented that juncture where it became possible for one digital rhythm to be mixed with different voices multiple times over to provide a sub-genre of dancehall songs all on the same rhythm. This was followed by the production of many popular "riddims" (rhythms) that featured the voices of countless dancehall artistes voicing their own particular brand of dancehall artistry over the same digital rhythm. The names of these rhythms also spoke and continue to speak to the social and cultural life of Jamaica. Popular dancehall rhythms include UnMetered Taxi, Party Time, Showtime, Nine Night, Log On, Online, Juice and Diwali.

The development and spread of dancehall as a unique musical and cultural form was aided by the symbiotic development and maintenance of popular sound systems like the immortal Stone Love Movements, Aces, Inner City, Metro Media, Kilamanjaro, Roadstar and Pieces. These mobile sound systems provided and continue to provide the first real stage and outlet for the performances of aspiring deejays and singers. These aspirants would attach themselves to a popular sound system and travel across the country to dances where they (might) get a chance to "chat pon di mike" (talk on the microphone) at a dance event and thus air their lyrical prowess to the discriminating dancehall audience. Many

Wayne "Sleng Teng" Smith performing at Heat in De Place Concert, Kingston, July 1985. Courtesy of the Gleaner Company Limited.

of these aspiring artistes often "buss out" (burst out) as performing stars in the dancehall, locally and globally.[46] Today, the role of sound systems and discos in the cultural production and promotion of dancehall music and culture remains paramount but not primary. The club scene and, more specifically, the local, regional and international media are now more particularly intertwined with the production, promotion and spread of the lyrics and culture of the dancehall and correspondingly the growth and maintenance of the careers of aspiring artistes.

The development of Jamaica's media landscape from the late 1980s though the 1990s aided in the spread of dancehall while the liberalization of the electronic media moved Jamaica away from reliance on two radio sources – Radio Jamaica and the Rediffusion Network (RJR) and Jamaica Broadcasting Corporation (JBC) and their subsidiaries – to newer players on the horizon. By 1990, following the divestment of the media environment in the 1980s, two new players were added to this arena – KLAS 89 out of Mandeville and Hot 102 (formerly Radio Waves) out of Montego Bay. The introduction of Irie FM ("Reggae Radio") in 1991 resulted in the erosion of RJR's "Supreme Sound" and JBC's Radio 1 monopoly and hegemony. By 1994, Irie FM's development of a programme schedule built almost entirely around popular reggae and dancehall music eventually netted it increasingly high levels of audience listenership. In late 1991, RJR Supreme Sound controlled 42.2 per cent to Irie FM's 20.4 per cent of the overall station shares. By early 1995, Irie FM's station shares had increased to 29.5 per cent, even as RJR Supreme Sound's shares decreased to 30.7 per cent of overall station shares for that period.[47]

The introduction of two other radio stations, Power 106 and Love FM, and their access to overall station shares deserves recognition; however, Irie FM's increasing competition for and access to market shares in radio was directly linked to its the use of popular reggae and dancehall music to generate and maintain high audience levels. In this regard, Irie FM made a significant contribution to the increasing output of popular reggae and dancehall music on local radio. Today, Jamaica boasts a total of fifteen radio stations.[48] The competitive radio industry continues to ensure publicity for dancehall music and culture through its dissemination of music, lyrics and styles and the use of dancehall slang and music in advertisements.

The Jamaican television industry also benefited from liberalization during this era. It moved from dependence on JBC TV, a single government-subsidized national television station, to the introduction of two other national stations, CVM TV and LOVE TV, and the repositioning and renaming of JBC TV to TVJ. This was complemented by the regulation of the informal cable television industry in 1995 and the subsequent mandate to the cable providers to provide a local channel for community use. Many of these local cable channels featured large segments of dancehall events as well as dancehall videos as their main programming. Additionally, North American television stations, in particular BET and MTV, also aided in the spread of dancehall music and culture by promoting dancehall music and videos as a part of their exclusive focus on music and entertainment. In Jamaica, the convergence of dancehall music, culture and television was cemented in 2003 with the introduction of Jamaica's RE (Reggae Entertainment) TV and HYPE (How You Perceive Entertainment) TV on the local cable network in Jamaica. Both stations maintain an exclusive focus on Jamaican music and entertainment with dancehall music and culture representing more than 80 per cent of their output.[49]

Indeed, since its development as a thriving part of Jamaica's informal sector, the dancehall continues to operate as an (informal) economic space in a capitalist, free-market environment. In so doing, the economic space of dancehall persistently encourages small-scale entrepreneurship and provides a thriving source of income for a variety of groupings and individuals – many of whom originate among the urban poor. These income-generating activities include prominent and publicized careers as performing artistes or deejays and other lucrative work as songwriters, dancehall models, dancers, promoters, producers, sound system operators, videographers, photographers, small vendors (soup, liquor, peanuts, cane, cigarettes, marijuana and so on), tailors, dressmakers, hairdressers, barbers and clothing store operators. While the Jamaican motto holds out the promise of full equality with its conciliatory "Out of Many, One People" rhetoric, the traditionally con-

Within minutes of a dancehall session or stage show such as Sting or Sunsplash, patrons can buy a clean audiotaped copy from an informal vendor. Here, a "tapeman" or "cassette hawk" showcases his wares in Kingston, May 1993. Courtesy of the Gleaner Company Limited.

stricted socioeconomic and political class hierarchy in Jamaica operates to ensure that many of these informal entrepreneurs are denied any real access to meaningful resources because of their lower-class origin or identification. In this instance, therefore, dancehall culture provides its actors with real economic tools for their attack on and revolution against the confining superstructure of traditional Jamaican society.

The dancehall is extremely visible and pervasive in Jamaican popular culture and society. It is loud and colourful. Its heavy bass, catchy slang, flashy regalia, colourful and daring costumes, vibrant dances, and defiantly arrogant attitudes are hard to miss. Over the last two decades, dancehall music and culture have slyly incorporated themselves into Jamaican television and radio advertisements, news programmes and newspaper articles; its flashy slang skims across the dialogue of entranced Jamaican youths. Dancehall posters blaze colour and hype across visual spaces and its overall noise and publicity is a riot that continuously disturbs the peace. The oral, aural and visual intensity of dancehall culture guarantees that many individuals from different socioeconomic backgrounds consume dancehall culture both consciously and unconsciously, willingly and unwillingly, as they carry out their day-to-day activities in Jamaica. Dancehall music and culture is constantly engaged in a battle for space in the land of its birth.

From its early development in the 1980s, the trend of the Yellowman-type slack and vulgar lyrics married to the "gun tunes" and gangsta lyrics, its cultural output (music, lyrics, slang, dances, styles, postures and fashions) has been perceived as distasteful by the gatekeepers of culture in Jamaica whose homogenization and strident denunciation of this "vulgar, sexual, ghetto culture" has dogged the dancehall.

Dancehall culture has been labelled "disgusting", "violent", "horrible", and the deejays' behaviour as "boorish, crass, coarse and primitive" by prominent members of Jamaican society.[50] The moral panic extends to the point where dancehall has been identified as one main contributor to both the high levels of violent crime in Jamaica and the poor grades earned by high-school boys.[51] Indeed, the dancehall has been credited with wide-ranging social, sociological and ideological potential to affect Jamaican culture negatively.[52] Many of these guardians of Jamaica's "high culture" perceive the dancehall as a degenerate and vulgar parody of music and culture where dancehall lyrics, music and fashions replicate the hardened and offensive sensibilities as well as the overt sexuality of the unwashed masses that exist on the fringes of Jamaican society.[53] This bias has formed a critical part of the dialogue, commentary and dismissal of dancehall music (sometimes referred to as "ragga") and its cultural sphere, and has severely limited the range of analytical and critical work done on this cultural product. Beyond doubt, from an early beginning with Carolyn Cooper's celebratory feminist focus on eroticism in her textual and lyrical analyses of Jamaican dancehall culture,[54] published academic analysis of early dancehall music culture has remained sparse. The overwhelming moralizing and sermonizing on dancehall music and culture that underpin the traditional moral panic of the educated and middle classes emanate predominantly from journalistic endeavours which are often balanced with others that use a similar medium to identify or analyse the dancehall. Examples of this ongoing debate are found in newspaper columns and letters to the editor in the daily and weekly Jamaican newspapers, in particular the *Jamaica Gleaner,* the *Jamaica Observer* and the *Star* newspapers.[55] Consequently, Jamaican newspapers remain one of the most valuable resources for academic research on social and political responses to and perceptions of dancehall music and culture in Jamaica.

The long-overdue coming of age of what I term the "dancehall generation" in the academy in the late 1990s has resulted in a growing body of work that moves away from the demonizing, infantilizing and romanticizing that has characterized earlier debates on the dancehall. These works critically examine Jamaican dancehall music and culture, and represent a progressive trend in the unmasking of the multiple factors at work in the dancehall space.[56] They move beyond text-based interpretations towards delineating a holistic view of dancehall culture and they include interdisciplinary approaches and interrogations that centre on dancehall creators, performers and performances in their own respective spheres.

University academic Carolyn Cooper argued from early on that the overt slackness of the dancehall deejay is "potentially a politics of subversion, a metaphorical revolt against law and order; an undermining of consensual standards of decency".[57] For Cooper, dancehall further represents "a radical, underground confrontation with the patriarchal gender ideology and the pious morality of fundamentalist Jamaican society".[58] It is undeniable that the majority of dancehall artistes represent the voice of the "downtown", that is, the dispossessed masses of Jamaica who operate in a dichotomous space that contends with the values and mores of the traditional "uptown", that is, the Jamaican middle and upper classes. However, based on my work, I argue that this revolt from the underbelly of Jamaican popular culture fails to confront the patriarchal gender ideology that underpins Jamaican gender relations. (See, in particular, chapter 3 of this work.)

It is, however, undeniable that the regular and ongoing controversy that forms a major part of the discussions of traditional Jamaica about the dancehall also ensures dancehall's continued access to wide-scale media publicity. The most noticeable high points of these controversies are generally around the staging of the now defunct Reggae Sunsplash and its successor, Reggae Sumfest, taking place during late July or early August, as well as around the annual staging of the popular dancehall event entitled Sting, held on 26 December. Dancehall music and culture have been and continue to be alternately reviled for their slackness and crass materialism while simultaneously commended for their pragmatic approach to existential reality. For some, dancehall music culture is a subculture best subdued, while for others it is both a response to and a re-presentation of Jamaican society from the late 1980s to the present. My own critical examination of the dancehall reveals social, political, economic and cultural linkages between dancehall culture and partisan political violence, political garrisons, donmanship, illegal drug culture, gun culture and gun violence in Jamaica.[59] I also reveal linkages with Jamaican oral and popular culture, African traditions, traditional patri- archy and gender politics, and the traditional sphere of Jamaica's socio- economic structures.

While the debate ebbs and flows, actors in dancehall culture have suc- cessfully created a space that legitimizes and gives authority to symbols and ideologies that are often positioned in direct opposition to the tra- ditional norms and mores of Jamaica. Indeed, the norms, mores and pre- ferred values of the dancehall dis/place serve to reflect and reinforce the lived realities of its adherents and, further, to legitimize their personhood and social identities. The dancehall also encapsulates a dynamic eco- nomic space within which actors can access and utilize economic resources. The symbols and ideologies within the dancehall dis/place serve as personal tools of liberation and avenues towards obtaining per- sonal freedom for many who exist within or subscribe to its "slack", "loud" and "vulgar" space – the hype, "bashment" and "bling bling"[60] that is the space of the dancehall. The norms and values at work in the dancehall create a space within which inner-city, lower-class and work- ing-class identities and notions of personhood are granted the legitimacy and acceptance that are denied its actors in the wider framework of traditional Jamaican society, all while simultaneously constituting a contradictory mix of positives and negatives. Consequently, the undisputed flowering of creative talent in the dancehall is a radical example of identity negotiation which reflects a new sense of self-acceptance, confidence and positive self-images at the base of society since many dancehall deejays and artistes hail from inner cities and lower-income households. Their forms of creative expression increasingly reflect local culture, values and styles and a new kind of self-confidence that revolts against the traditional ascriptions of identity and social position that fortify Jamaica's rigid class structure.

Reggae music of the type promoted internationally by Bob Marley has been viewed as one of the more revolutionary forms of music coming out of a Caribbean with a history of slavery and colonialism.[61] Reggae music has been perceived as social commentary, yes, but also in its every thought, verse and musical pulse, as reflecting survival, accommodation, revolution and the daily realities of the children of the diaspora. Like reggae music culture, its predecessor and close relative, dancehall music culture also incorporates revolutionary sites, that is, sites of resistance and struggle against the traditional social order. The transition from reggae to dancehall in Jamaican music represented a shift in the terrain of culture "towards popular, everyday practices and local narratives; and towards the decentring of old hierarchies and grand narratives".[62] Aided by global factors including digitization, the rise and proliferation of new media, as well as market demand, dancehall artistes have been able to articulate their narrative discourses and project their images and localized representations across and beyond the inner cities of Kingston and St Andrew into the national spaces of Jamaica and outwards to the global spaces of the Jamaican and African diaspora. To this end, while it may both be affected by and encapsulate elements of earlier forms of Jamaican music (for example, mento, ska, dub, roots rock and reggae), the music culture labelled "dancehall" occupies a cultural, political, ideological and economic space in Jamaica that is marked by late-twentieth-century developments and has a definite point of disjuncture with preceding manifestations of popular Jamaican music culture. Dancehall music culture is a conjunctural moment in Jamaican society, with its own historical specificity. While it exhibits similarities and continuities with other historically relevant moments, it cannot be and is not the same moment.[63] Therefore, for the purposes of this work, I assert that dancehall music and culture utilized and still utilize extreme manifestations of social, cultural, political and economic issues that are particular to the late twentieth and now the twenty-first century. Therefore, dancehall remains simultaneously linked to but critically exiled from all preceding genres of Jamaican music culture. Dancehall culture maintains its own historical specificity.

Indeed, since Bob Marley's international success as Jamaica's premier reggae artiste, dancehall has proven the most commercially successful form of Jamaican music to date. Reggae dancehall artistes like Shabba Ranks (winner of the Grammy for Best Reggae Album in 1991 and 1992), Patra, Cobra, Super Cat, Chaka Demus & Pliers, Beenie Man (winner of the Grammy for Best Reggae Album in 2000), Bounty Killer, Shaggy (winner of the Grammy for Best Reggae Album in 1995), Sean Paul (winner of the Grammy for Best Reggae Album in 2003), Wayne Wonder and Elephant Man, among others, have successfully broken into the Japanese, European and North American markets and have continued to ensure the global spread of reggae dancehall music and its associated images. Witter estimates the income accruing to Jamaicans from the music industry to be "in the order of US$60–100 million, which would make it more important to the Jamaican economy than sugar as a foreign exchange earner".[64]

Contemporary dancehall culture is a cultural site for the creation and dissemination of symbols and ideologies that reflect and legitimize the lived realities of its adherents. Many of its more prominent creators and artistes originate in the inner cities and poorest communities of Kingston, St Andrew and St Catherine in Jamaica, and the dancehall increasingly symbolizes the existential realities and struggles of individuals in these communities. I argue in the following chapter that the dancehall is a cultural dis/place of ongoing dialogue, confrontation and contestation with the rigid sociopolitical, gendered class hierarchies of Jamaica. Its multiple discourses encode the negotiations of gendered structures of power, heavy emphasis on sexuality and sex play, and deep linkages with political violence, garrisons, donmanship, illegal drug culture, gun culture and (gun) violence in Jamaica, which are all exemplified in the movies

Dancehall Queen and *Third World Cop*. The explosive creativity and cunning adaptability of dancehall music and culture has ensured its continuity as "a field of active cultural production, a means by which black lower-class youth articulate and project a distinct identity in local, national, and global contexts"[65] for over two decades.

The transformations in the economic sector, changes in urban trends and the rise of the informal economy since the early 1980s impacted on access to wealth and the corresponding access to economic markers of status by actors from lower socioeconomic backgrounds. These individuals including ICIs, deejays, traders in foreign exchange on the black market, traders in illegal drugs, among others, were able to access a great deal of wealth. This access to wealth and its many attendant markers of high social status are today effectively transforming the socioeconomic framework. This transformation is more problematic as status respectability and legitimacy in Jamaica has become increasingly defined by the acquisition and conspicuous consumption of more and more symbols of wealth. These symbols include luxury motor vehicles; expensive jewellery; expensive brand-name clothing and accessories; frequent trips to foreign countries; residences in apartment buildings, up-scale townhouse complexes or large houses in prime residential areas as well as ownership and conspicuous use of late-model cellular phones.

In this highly materialistic framework, the most prominent, publicized and visible creators and disseminators of the flashy dancehall culture and hype – the deejays, dancers and models – are also the most conspicuous consumers of their newly earned wealth. These men and women have succeeded in conspicuously re-presenting themselves as ideals and have arguably become newer, shinier role models for Jamaican youths from different socioeconomic backgrounds. Further, as access to economic wealth through formal channels becomes more difficult and less financially rewarding in many instances, the once ideal careers of lawyer, doctor or teacher are facing obsolescence as generally accepted models of success. Many young men and women perceive a career as a deejay or promoter in the informal dancehall sector as more accessible, legitimate and having greater and quicker capacity to earn large amounts of wealth than those in the formal sector.

However, many dancehall superstars who come equipped with their lyrical fusillades and bashment hype under the brilliantly lit scopes of the willing videographers who record their every word, gesture and gyration for posterity seem oblivious of the weight of social responsibility that has been thrust upon them by a society in transition. Instead, driven by a consumerist culture thriving in a free-market capitalist environment, they place more emphasis on their increased access to, and conspicuous consumption of, the symbols of status respectability than on their increasing impact on Jamaican society at home and in the diaspora. In fact, by its unconcerned behaviour and its pervasive, unstemmed hype, Jamaica's dancehall continues to expand and defy definition.

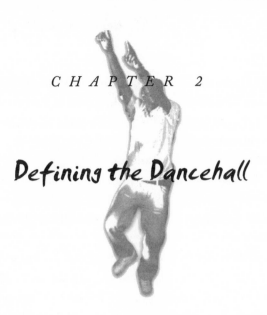

CHAPTER 2

Defining the Dancehall

THROUGHOUT THIS BOOK, I use the term dis/place to impute sociocultural and political meanings to the dancehall space. The identification of this space as the dis/place provides a framework within which I locate overlapping symbols of power and domination and the ongoing struggles within the dancehall. First, the word "displace" is defined in the *Concise Oxford Dictionary* as follows: "to shift from its place; remove from office; oust; take the place of; put something in the place of". Here, I argue that the dancehall dis/place operates as a site of revolution and transformation, effectively creating its own symbols and ideologies and negating, shifting, removing and replacing those functioning in the traditional sociopolitical spaces.

Second, I use the Jamaican creole term *dis* which is translated into English to mean "this". In this usage, dis/place refers to "this place" that is, this existential place or space. In this instance, the dancehall dis/place provides a mirror of the lived realities of its affectors and affectees and acts as social commentary on the negotiations and relationships within and beyond the immediate space of the dancehall.

Third, the term encapsulates the sociopolitically loaded meaning of the Jamaican creole "dis", a slang term used in both dancehall culture and broader Jamaican society where it is an abbreviation of the word "disrespect" and its derivatives. For example, "Da bwoy deh dis mi"

(That boy [man] committed an act of disrespect against my person).

Issues of identity and status play a key role in dancehall culture and its symbiotic relationship with inner-city culture. Actors, who are precariously placed economically and sociopolitically and who are intent on redefining their ascribed roles and claiming higher levels of wealth, respect and authority by any means, are more defensive and protective of their perceived status. In this dynamic space, "dis" is translated as a perceived act of disrespect committed against an individual's status or identity. A "dis", whether perceived or real, usually results in retaliatory violence, which may be on a continuum from a simple string of loud curse words (badwords) to the extreme act of murder. Often, the reaction of the "dissed" individual may not parallel the seeming slight that has been identified as a "dis". For example, an unsuspecting man who makes sexual overtures to the woman of a highly respected don will often have to pay with his life.

Consequently, dis/place as used herein refers to "this disrespectful place where we have been placed"; "this place where we are consistently disrespected and mistreated"; "this place where we are consistently denied our legitimate human rights"; "this place where we are denied access to resources"; "this place where our identities are negated" and, even more importantly, "this place from within which we are forced to re-create and claim our resources, identities, personhood and self-esteem by any means".

Throughout this work any usage of the term dis/place imputes any one, any combination or all of the foregoing meanings, particularly where dis/place is combined with the term dancehall.

What Is "Dancehall"?

Originally, the term "dancehall" was used to describe a place or "hall" used for the staging of dances and similar events. There is no general consensus on how the term became identified with this form of Jamaican popular culture. One can speculate that the proliferation of stage shows and other staged events backed by the sound systems resulted in dancehall's identification as a music that is tied to a space and place. However, dancehall music can be defined as that genre of Jamaican popular music that originated in the early 1980s. The contemporary manifestation of dancehall music culture is more than simply a composite of all music genres that have existed in Jamaica since slavery. Indeed, all genres of popular Jamaican music since slavery have been labelled and positioned in their respective historical, social, economic and political frameworks. While affected by and encapsulating elements of earlier forms of Jamaican music (for example, mento, ska, dub, roots rock and reggae), the music culture labelled "dancehall" occupies a late-twentieth-century cultural, political, ideological and economic space in Jamaica and has a definite point of disjuncture with preceding manifestations of popular Jamaican music culture. Because of its extreme manifestations of social, cultural, political and economic issues that are particular only to the late twentieth century, dancehall music culture is critically exiled from all preceding genres of Jamaican music culture. Like Rastafari reggae music, dancehall music culture may encapsulate some elements of the preceding forms of music culture but it simultaneously creates an entirely new form from a cornucopia of elements that exist in its contemporary space. In short, the label "dancehall" must remain positioned in and affixed to this late twentieth century space in Jamaican popular music and culture. The deejays, sound systems, stage shows, club scene and energetic dances are key elements that inform the foundation of the performative space of the dancehall and the lived realities of the dancehall creators and adherents.

Contemporary dancehall music and its cultural dis/place have become more than the sum total of the popularized lyrical output of its most prominent artistes, the deejays. Dancehall culture is a space for the cultural creation and dissemination of symbols and ideologies that reflect and legitimize the lived realities of its adherents, particularly those from the inner cities of Jamaica. Because many of its more prominent creators, artistes and adherents originated or were socialized in these poverty-stricken inner-city communities, the dancehall increasingly symbolizes the existential struggles of individuals in these communities. In fact, the dancehall dis/place is an arena for the creation, re-creation and dissemination of symbols that serve to legitimize and reinforce this lived existence and this is characterized by strong links to extra-legal and illegal actors and activities. The dancehall dis/place is where its creators and adherents articulate and narrate their conceptions of self; it is the arena where popular and legitimated images of personhood are parodied and performed. It is "where we discover and play with the identifications of ourselves, where we are imagined, where we are represented, not only to the audiences out there who do not get the message, but to ourselves for the first time".[1]

Although the deejays and dancers/models have historically been the most publicized actors in the dancehall, its adherents cannot be defined as a homogeneous group.[2] Based on my own research, I find it prudent, therefore, to outline some categories or typologies of heterogeneous actors (affectors and affectees) who operate within dancehall culture.

Categories or Typologies of Affectors and Affectees

I use the two broad terms "affectors" and "affectees" to outline the heterogeneous nature of the actors within dancehall culture. The categories and subcategories within these two broad headings each represent a composite of a larger identity group. They do not, however, claim to be mutually exclusive, nor do they purport to encompass all the identity groups and consumers of dancehall culture. As a matter of fact, there are significant leakages between these two broad categories as well as within the subgroups that make up each category.

Affectors are primarily creators of dancehall culture and affectees are primarily consumers of dancehall culture. However, because of the symbiotic nature of popular culture in general, and dancehall culture in particular, many affectors and affectees are simultaneously creators and consumers. Nonetheless, particular groups are either engaged primarily in the creation or the consumption of dancehall's output. Therefore, based on their level of creation or consumption, these groups are classified either as affectors or affectees with a line of demarcation between the two.

The Affectors: Creators of Dancehall Culture

The composite categories or typologies of affectors that I have identified are song creators, sound system operators, promoters/producers, dynamic hype creators, visual creators and deejays.

Song creators engage in the creation of the lyrics and the rhythms that form the foundation of dancehall music. It is important to note that many deejays (categorized in the following) do not compose all the lyrics for the songs that make up their repertoire. The creative licence for the rhythms and lyrics of the dancehall often lies in the hands of individuals who prefer to remain hidden from the public hype and bashment of dancehall culture.

Sound system operators own and/or operate the mobile sound systems that travel locally, regionally and internationally to provide music and hype for dancehall events. Wee Pow, owner of Stone Love, one of dancehall's most popular sound systems, is an important example.

Promoters/producers provide the economic backing and support for the staging and promotion of dancehall events, the promotion of dancehall artistes and the dissemination of dancehall music locally, regionally and internationally.

Dynamic hype creators are the male and female models, dancers and slang creators in dancehall culture. The dancehall model is involved in the dynamic creation/re-creation and display of fashion styles that inevitably affect the appearance of the consumers. The dancehall dancer engages in dynamic creation/re-creation and display of dancehall dance styles that are inevitably imitated by dancehall consumers. Female dancers usually engage in erotic and sexual displays as part of their dance styles. These dance styles are usually (but not always) driven by the creation of a new rhythm or song in the dancehall as well as by social and political developments in Jamaican society and the international arena. The slang creator engages in the dynamic creation/re-creation and dissemination of slang that is inevitably imitated by dancehall consumers. This slang is, more often than not, subsequently used in dancehall songs and is then picked up by sections of the wider society, especially the youths. Although one subject may function exclusively as a model, dancer or slang creator, others may simultaneously function in two or all three of these areas. Dancehall's late master dancer and icon, Bogle (Gerald Levy, 1964–2005) is a key example of a dynamic hype creator. Bogle's consummate dance prowess, his dramatic style of dress, and his consistent development of dance-hall slang and dance styles indelibly mark his passage through the dancehall dis/place.

Visual creators engage in activities that result in the creation and dissemination of visual images of the dancehall culture. This dissemination is both within and beyond the boundaries of the dancehall subculture at the one end and Jamaica's physical boundaries at the other end. This group includes two subcategories:

The late master dancer and hype producer Bogle (Gerald Levy) poses inside Miles Enterprises at the weekly hype dancehall event Passa Passa Wednesdays, April 2004. Donna P. Hope photo.

1. *Moving visual creators,* who create and disseminate audiovisual representations of the dancehall culture, including documentaries, television programmes, news clips and dancehall videos.

2. *Still visual creators,* who create and disseminate still images of the dancehall culture. These still images may or may not be driven by written text. These include photographs, newspaper articles and magazine articles.

Self-taught dancehall videographer Jack Sowah (Courtney Cousins), owner of Sowah Productions, is a popular moving visual creator, while photographer Horseman is a noted still visual creator in the dancehall dis/place.

Deejays/DJs are engaged in the oral performance of dancehall music. One should note that many deejays also function as song creators and promoters/producers. Deejays include several subcategories, a few of which are as follows:

1. *Girls dem deejay*: This subcategory is defined as the male deejay who chiefly engages in the performance of songs that focus on women and their sexuality. This focus may include heightened praise of female voluptuousness, sexual prowess, sexual fidelity, tolerance of male infidelity, financial independence, among others. Because of the heavy emphasis on overt descriptions and depictions of sex, female sexuality and sex organs, the output from this category of deejays generally includes a high proportion of songs that are banned from broadcast on the mainstream media and designated "not fit for airplay". Examples of a girls dem deejay include King Yellowman and Shabba Ranks.

2. *Slackness deejay*: This subcategory is defined as the deejay who chiefly engages in the performance and dissemination of songs that are perceived and labelled as sexually explicit, lewd and vulgar. This subcategory may often, but not always, cut across the above category of the girls dem deejay. The output of the slackness deejay includes a high proportion of songs designated "not fit for airplay". Examples include King Yellowman, Lady Saw and Shabba Ranks.

3. *Bad-man deejay*: This subcategory is defined as the deejay who engages chiefly in the dissemination of songs containing graphic descriptions of perceived violent and criminal acts, including illegal gun- and drug-related activity. The ideological orientation of this deejay is usually evidenced by his style of dress as well as his facial contortions and menacing body language during onstage perform-ances. The bad-man deejay is often involved in behaviours and practices that are labelled deviant and violent during his offstage interactions. His output includes songs designated "not fit for airplay" because of the pervasiveness of threatening, ominous and violence-laden symbols and images in these songs. Deejays who fit into this category include Ninjaman, Josey Wales, Bounty Killer and Super Cat.

4. *Rastafari deejay:* A Rastafari deejay overtly subscribes to the religious ideology and world view of Rastafari. This religious orientation is usually reflected in the content of the majority of the songs which he or she performs and disseminates, the physical appearance of the subject (including his or her wearing of dreadlocks and Rastafari regalia) and the lifestyle of the deejay. This individual is differentiated from those contemporary deejays who adopt the wearing of dreadlocks as a hairstyle and not as an outward manifestation of their conversion to the Rastafari faith (that is, of sighting Rastafari). Examples of this group include Capleton, Anthony B and Sizzla. I noted earlier that while this category of deejay plays an important role in dancehall music and culture and is mentioned throughout this work, the category will not be discussed in great detail.

5. *All-rounder deejay:* This subcategory is defined as the deejay who engages in the performance and dissemination of songs that cut across all the foregoing categories without focusing on any one category. The all-rounder deejay often engages in various collaborative efforts with regional and international artistes and ensures the cross-fertilization of dancehall music and culture with the music and culture of related black diasporan cultural forms like North American hip-hop. Examples include Beenie Man, Elephant Man and Baby Cham.

The Affectees: Consumers of Dancehall Culture

The composite categories or typologies of dancehall affectees that I have identified are separated into gendered groups as follows: the female categories are Miss Hotty Hotty, Miss Vogue, Miss Thing and independent ooman/big ooman. The male categories are don/shotta, don youth/yute, freaky hype type and big man/dads/faada/heavy man.

Miss Hotty Hotty is a younger woman between sixteen and thirty-five years old. She generally hails from the inner city, lower-middle- or lower-class background. Her education is generally limited to the secondary level and she may be only functionally literate, but she is "street smart". She is employed, underemployed or self-employed in an informal activity. Many are partially or totally dependent on a man for economic resources. Most are mothers and are unmarried. In the dancehall, these women prefer expensive hairstyles and accessories with brand-name clothing. Those who cannot afford the real thing will go to great pains to get custom-made copies of popular styles. Many of these women prefer tight, short and revealing costumes which accentuate their sexuality. They are all heterosexual and anti-homosexual. Many of these women have been popularized as dancehall queens because of their preference for tight, revealing, flamboyant costumes and their propensity to "skin out" and display their bodies in erotic poses at dancehall events.

Miss Vogue is a younger woman between sixteen and thirty-five years old. She hails from the lower middle, middle or upper classes. She is usually very literate and has completed secondary-level education. She may also be completing or have completed studies at the tertiary level and may hold professional qualifications or certification. She may be pursuing a professional career or employed in the corporate world. Miss Vogue prefers expensive clothes and accessories. She will often "dress down" in less flamboyant costumes like jeans and t-shirts while maintaining a costly aura. Most of these women have no children and some are married. Excessive displays of sexuality are usually avoided. She is heterosexual, but not violently anti-homosexual.

Miss Thing is a young woman between eighteen and thirty years old. She hails from the lower classes or from the inner city. More often than not she has made great strides in advancing herself economically and socially. She last attended school at the secondary level but is interested in advancing herself educationally. Miss Thing is generally a dancehall model, dancer or artiste or owns and operates a small business enterprise such as a clothing store that caters to the dancehall hype, a hairdressing salon or some type of cosmetology establishment. Most of these women have no children and they prefer to dress in expensive, flashy and revealing costumes and expensive jewellery. Many prefer to have liaisons with powerful and wealthy men who can assist in their quest for social and economic mobility. As a general rule, Miss Thing ensures that her car keys are prominently displayed at dancehall events. She is heterosexual, but not overtly concerned about homosexuality.

The independent ooman/big ooman is a middle-aged to older woman who is in her mid-thirties to late fifties or early sixties. She is often from the inner city or lower class with a few hailing from the lower middle class. The independent ooman may have completed the secondary level and may sometimes hold some professional qualification or certification. Tertiary education is rare. The independent ooman is usually self-employed or is an entrepreneur (for example, ICI, hairdresser, dressmaker, nail technologist or other cosmetologist, professional). These women prefer brand-name clothing, flashy jewellery, expensive hairstyles and accessories. They are overtly heterosexual and anti-homosexual. Many are in full control of their sexuality and often prefer male partners who are much younger.

The don youth/yute is a man who is aged between eighteen and thirty-eight years. He is usually from the lower middle, middle or upper classes. He has usually completed secondary education and may have some tertiary training or is either engaged in or plans to commence this level. Many are self-employed, engaged in family business, pursuing a professional career or attending school. A don youth/yute prefers understated but expensive brand-name clothing and accessories. He is usually heterosexual and generally less concerned with homosexuality.

The don/shotta is a man who may range between twenty-two and sixty years old. He generally comes from the inner city, lower classes or the lower middle classes. He may have completed the secondary level of education and a small percentage may have some tertiary training. He may be an entrepreneur or is self-employed in various enterprises. These include legal, extra-legal or illegal commercial or other business activities. In some instances, the don/shotta may have strong, partisan political linkages to the JLP or PNP. He prefers brand-name clothing and accessories and may gravitate towards the classy look of the formal three-piece suit. He wears conspicuous and expensive jewellery. He may hold a licensed firearm which he takes great pains to display. He is promiscuously heterosexual and violently anti-homosexual.

The freaky hype type is usually at least fifteen years old with no age limit. His socioeconomic background and status is varied but the greater majority come from the inner cities or lower working classes. The freaky hype type usually has some secondary education and a few may have done some tertiary studies. Many of these men dress conspicuously in elaborate stylized costumes. The freaky hype type pays careful attention to his hairstyle and many of them sport fancy, complicated corn-row designs or some other colourful and elaborate hairstyle. He is clean-shaven and slim-bodied and pays careful attention to facial and bodily aesthetics. He often travels as part of a group that is responsible for the hype and excitement that characterizes the dancehall dance, club or stage show event. Many of these men are underemployed or unemployed and depend on a female relative or partner for their sustenance. Oftentimes, his elaborate and expensive costumes are gifts from family members who live abroad. Many of these men exhibit great prowess in the dynamic dance styles that are an important part of the dancehall. Since the late 1990s, there has been a steady increase in individuals who fit into this category.

The big man/dads/fada/heavy man is usually between thirty and sixty years old. His background is lower class or lower middle class and in some instances he may hail from the inner cities. He has completed secondary level and may have some tertiary education. He is self-employed, engaged in family business or pursuing a professional career. Like the don/shotta, he may have strong partisan, political linkages but this is rare. He prefers understated but expensive brand-name clothing and accessories and small amounts of expensive jewellery. He may hold a legal firearm and is promiscuously heterosexual and often aggressively and vocally anti-homosexual.

The related themes of gender and sexuality run through the foregoing typologies of dancehall affectors and affectees. During my research, the dialogue and narratives of the affectors and the actions, mode of dress and general orientation of the affectees underscored the dis/place's pre-occupation with gender and sexuality as sites of identity negotiation in dancehall culture. This passionate engagement and its images are explored and analysed in the following chapter on gender and sexuality.

CHAPTER 3

"Love Punaany Bad":
Sexuality and Gender in the Dancehall

GENDER POLITICS AND patriarchy remain vibrant parts of the dancehall. They filter through what has often been labelled vulgar, slack, sexually explicit, misogynist and anti-homosexual lyrics. These lyrics, however, reveal much more than a subculture or group actively engaged in the spread of sexually explicit, misogynist and anti-homosexual lyrics. The existence of these, together with what has been labelled homophobia in the dancehall, is really part of a cultural dialogue of gendered identity that draws on the historical and cultural legacies of Jamaica. This cultural dialogue highlights several core issues affecting not only the masculine and feminine identities in the dancehall dis/place, but also the broader masculine and feminine identities in Jamaica.

Gender/Race/Colour

Social construction theories outline gendering as a process where men and women are identified at birth and then assigned particular sex roles and gendered expectations. A child is labelled male or female based on the identification of the male or female sex organs[1] and this sets the individual in a gendered category for a lifetime. This process, which is located in the socially constructed binary of male and female difference

36

and sex roles, passes itself off as "naturally" rooted in biology. This belief that gender polarization is a "natural and inevitable consequence of the intrinsic biological natures of women and men" is referred to by Bem[2] as "biological essentialism". Beginning at birth, it is a process that structures the entire life of the individual labelled "man" or "woman". Gender roles are, therefore, also social constructs encompassing self-concepts, psychological traits, as well as class, family, occupational, historical and political roles assigned to each sex. Gender is therefore also defined as "the social organization of sexual difference"[3] where it is an innate something that a man or woman has. Gender is not only bio-logically determined, but is more a socially constructed category created for the ranking of maleness and femaleness.

In postcolonial societies such as Jamaica, gender stratification oper-ates in a framework of patriarchy that can be clearly defined as a system or society reflecting values underpinning the traditional male ideal. It is masculism in a political context and it is supported by all the institu-tions operating within that system or society. Patriarchy is not only male dominance in its strictest sense, but also a persistent ideology of male superordination that both men and women maintain consciously and unconsciously. In this system, both men and women are victims, how-ever, a male hegemonic world-view ranks and rewards men over women on the basis of gender. Patriarchy as a system produces and reproduces a set of personal, social and economic relationships that enable men to have power over women and the services they provide.[4]

In examining the social construction of gender roles in the anglophone Caribbean, however, feminist and gender theorists give credence to other factors that arise from the particular historical experiences of these societies and which also impact on the construction of gender roles and the operation of the system of patriarchy.[5] Slavery is one important historical experience on which rests the foundation of contemporary ide-ologies and relations of Afro-Caribbean societies like Jamaica. Both elites and masters as well as labourers and slaves in these Caribbean societies were affected by a cultural action or social process that incor-porated the dominant Eurocentric and the subordinate African elements of the society.[6] In the creolized societal mix that resulted from African slavery and European colonialism, race and class have been identified as the two dominant factors intersecting with gender. Consequently, among the historical legacies of slavery, indentureship, colonialism and post-colonialism, creolized issues of sexuality and identity were effectively tied to the race/class (colour) and gender hierarchy. Beginning around the sixteenth century, the process of defining women and non-whites as savage, uncontrollable and uncivilized provided an opening for the domestication and exploitation of these groups. Women and black people were credited with unnatural and insatiable sexual urges that needed the control and guidance of men – originally interpreted as white men. During Caribbean plantation slavery, white men were placed at the helm of the gendered sociopolitical hierarchy and black men and women were stereotyped as sexual animals, driven by insatiable sexual desires and in need of constant supervision. Indeed, both slavery and colonialism collapsed identities into sexed bodies, sexualizing Caribbean populations in racial terms and racializing them in sexual terms.

Therefore, ideological issues of sexuality and identity that were effectively tied to the race/class (colour) and gender hierarchy arose directly from the context of plantation slavery. In the Caribbean context of slavery, white men were placed at the helm. Notions of sex and sexuality were effectively created and perpetuated. The various acknowledged "colonised sexualities were essentially subordinated sexualities".[7] Myths were developed that fit neatly into the racist tenets that supported plantation society. For example, it was "common knowledge" that black women had no morals and were content to breed, dropping children almost at will; black women were strong like animals, they could work in the fields all day and then work in bed all night. Further, black women were seen as having insatiable and unnatural, animal-like sexual urges while black men were assumed to be well-endowed with large penises. Black men supposedly did not understand fatherhood in its Eurocentric sense and therefore preferred to have many women and many children. Of course, the myth was extended to the protection of the white female body where white women and their purity had to be safeguarded from the lustful attentions of insatiable black men. On the other hand, based on this sexualized falsehood, white men were also unsafe from the animal-like lust of black women, who were apparently capable of exerting some strange sexual hold. In short, black men and women were stereotyped as sexual animals driven by insatiable sexual desires. These sexualized and racialized beings were therefore in need of constant supervision by their white slave-owners and colonial masters.

Arising from this race and colour influenced society, a hierarchiy on the race-gender continuum in an Afro-Caribbean context such as Jamaica would be as follows:

1. White male
2. White female
3. Coloured male
4. Coloured female
5. Black male
6. Black female

A coloured man or woman is the bi-racial or multi-racial offspring of miscegenation. Historically, a black male would be allocated less power than a white or coloured female in this continuum. This has shifted somewhat in postcolonial, contemporary Caribbean society, driven by changes in the race/class/colour positionings based on access to resources and patterns of social mobility. Nevertheless, the working-class black woman is placed at the base of society and arguably remains so in the context of the contemporary Caribbean social organization – thrice denied by the vagaries of race, class and gender.[8] The ideal was and remains always that of the white male – the superordinate position on the race/class/gender continuum. This code of colour, what I like to refer to as "hierarchy of the skin", encodes the colour, racial and cultural distinctions of the neo-colonial order which places blacks at the base of the social hierarchy and whites at the apex.[9]

In Jamaica, gender hierarchies operate within a contemporary version of the racialized class system that developed out of slavery and colonialism. Concepts of beauty and ugliness and ideas of good speech or bad speech still depend on their closeness to what is a white, Eurocentric ideal. Even when it raises some debate, Jamaican women are reminded that beauty, as defined by the Miss Jamaica World and Miss Jamaica Universe beauty contests on an annual basis, still rests on a close approximation to the European phenotype.[10] Where sexuality is concerned, the Madonna/whore syndrome is transformed by these additional factors to produce the race- and class-influenced "ghetto slam" (ghetto sex) ideology. A man can get a ghetto slam from a *trang* (strong) black woman from the lower or working class or from the inner city – a black lower-working- class phenomenon. This woman is believed to have the physical make-up that makes her suitable for engagement in overtly physical displays of sexual activity – large breasts, large posterior, big frame. This is married to the lower socioeconomic positioning that makes her more accessible for use and/or abuse by men from different backgrounds. Beenie Man expresses this in his hit song "Slam":

> Gi mi di gyal dem wid di wickedest slam
> Di kind ah gyal who know how fi love up shi man
> Man if yuh want fi get di medal
> Yuh haffi get a slam from a real ghetto gyal
>
> (Give me the girls/women with the best sex
> The kind of girl/woman who knows how to love up her man
> Man! If you want to get the medal
> You have to have sex with a real ghetto girl/woman)

The "ghetto gyal's" oftentimes lighter-skinned, upper-/middle-class counterpart is often falsely perceived as less accessible and too "lady-like" and pure for engagement in any overtly physical displays of sexual prowess. As Jamaican concepts of feminine beauty consistently strive towards the European ideals of softness, clear skin, soft flowing hair – the *browning* or lighter-skinned woman continues to cop a higher place on the hierarchies of beauty and desirability in Jamaica. Many darker-skinned women resort to bleaching (if they are from the lower class); using dermatologist-approved skin lighteners (if they are of the middle/upper classes); or marrying (if they are of the middle/upper classes) into this ideal. Issues of colour and racial identity are still reflected in statements like "my ooman mus have hair pon har head" (my woman must have hair on her head) from men who link female beauty to unrealistic, Eurocentric ideals and therefore dismiss the low Afros that some Jamaican women prefer. Indeed, a woman who cannot lay claim to the soft, flowing tresses (be they natural, chemically altered or simply false extensions) that are defined as feminine in Jamaica's Eurocentric context is placed further down on the "look-good" chart and considered less than feminine by some. In an effort to obtain long, flowing hair, many women spend small fortunes on hairpieces, wigs and weaves.

The quest for the more socially accepted Eurocentric ideals of feminine beauty directly influences the late 1990s upsurge of skin bleaching by many inner-city women and men, who in Jamaica use illegal and often dangerous substances to lighten their skin colour in response to these pressures. Jamaican bleachers use a variety of steroid and lightening creams, like Ambi or Nadinola, and home-made concoctions, like toothpaste and bleach, to lighten their skin. Skin bleaching has been identified as a universal phenomenon that occurs wherever there is cultural domination.[11] In Jamaica, the phenomenon of skin bleaching is often coupled with the ingestion of the "fowl pill" by women to enhance their breast, hip and "bumper"[12] sizes. The "fowl pill" is the hormone tablet used to enhance the growth of chickens by chicken farmers in the broiler industry. However, women from the inner cities ingest these tablets and report that within a week, their breasts and bottoms increase in size. These increases are perceived as attractive in a context where the traditional and Eurocentric standards of beauty favour a *mawga* (skinny) woman. Paradoxically, large-bodied, full-breasted women are defined as attractive and sexy in inner-city culture and this is outlined in the lyrics, styles and discourses of dancehall culture. The politics of the body plays on a different field that is contained within, but separate from, the larger playing field of Jamaican life. I want to reiterate the point made earlier that it was in the dancehall that I first became aware of the sexual attractiveness of large, full-bodied, big-breasted women, affectionately called *mampy* or *mampy-size*. In the dancehall, these big, beautiful women are praised for their *trang* bodies and lauded because "dem nuh mawga and crawny". The fact that weight gain and body fat is equated with prosperity and social mobility and *mawganess* is equated with poverty and deprivation is a part of the politics that is played out across the bodies of these women. The dancehall as inner-city and lower-working-class culture encodes this fear of poverty and deprivation and negates its play across the bodies of its adherents while it simultaneously tackles the overarching dialogue of traditional Jamaica that places the slim-bodied woman at the helm of feminine beauty.

It is important to note the class biases that are inherent in these negotiations for space on the hierarchy of skin that bestows feminine beauty and higher status. Women and men from the lower classes and inner cities are usually accused of bleaching and become the subject of debates, panel discussions and papers from researchers and academics who focus on this "unnatural" practice which is often believed to speak to a lack of self-love and self-esteem. The official response from Jamaica's Ministry of Health was a campaign to confiscate the various medicated creams that were being sold over the counter or on the streets without a prescription.[13]

I participated in a panel discussion in 1999 put on by a group of final-year students at the Caribbean Institute of Media and Communication (CARIMAC) at the basic school in the Mona Commons community. Mona Commons is an inner-city community that is located close to the Mona campus of the University of the West Indies in Jamaica. The CARIMAC discussion was held under the theme "Loving the Skin You're In" and arose out of the then intense social debates about the upsurge of skin bleaching among inner-city residents. The most important moment in that seminar came when both male and female bleachers informed the university group that they were bleaching because it was a means of getting ahead in Jamaica. One woman opined that when you are lighter skinned, "yuh get more attention" and a young man declared that he intended to stop bleaching eventually but right now it was a "way out of the ghetto, cause people see you more when you brown". My own research in the dancehall has shown that many lower-class and inner-city residents who bleach have their own personal reasons why they do so which do not detract from their acceptance of their African heritage. They accept the truth of their Africanness but reject their darker skin colour because it is a hindrance to social mobility in colour-coded Jamaica. Indeed, the griots of the dancehall have consistently narrated these truths across the body of the dancehall, yet their words often go unheeded by well-meaning scholars and researchers.

The first time Buju Banton was invited onstage at Sting 1990 by Wayne Wonder, I stood and listened as he sang what would become his first popular dancehall song, "Browning": "Mi love mi cyar mi love mi bike mi love mi money an ting, / but most of all mi love mi brownin' "

A pre-Rastafari Buju Banton in a pleading pose at Reggae Sunsplash 1999.
Courtesy of the Gleaner Company Limited.

(I love my car, I love my bike, I love my money and all that, / but most
of all I love my lighter-skinned woman). The subsequent outcry from
"decent" Jamaica about the racial overtones of this song, forced Buju
Banton to hastily pen and release "Black Woman": "Mi nuh stop cry fi
all black woman, / love fi all di girls dem wid dark complexion" (I cannot stop lauding all black women, / praises for all the girls and women
with dark complexions).

Despite the "decent" protestations from traditional Jamaica, Buju's
"Browning" simply emphasized what Scott highlighted as the "Crowning of the Browning".[14] Buju, who had not yet been called to the Rastafari faith, idealized his browning over and above his car, his bike and his

money at that stage of his career because of his own internalization of the of social importance some Jamaicans attach to having a spouse with brown skin. The tensions between the quest to achieve the hegemonic ideal of near-whiteness and to move away from the lower-status dark skin colour is part of the identity debates in the dancehall where bleachers are lauded, jeered, denigrated or encouraged for their skin-lightening efforts.

For example, dancehall deejay Nardo Ranks, in his popular "Dem a Bleach", highlights this phenomenon thus: "Dem a bleach, dem a bleach out dem skin, / dem a bleach fi look like di browning" (They are bleaching, they are bleaching out their skins, / they are bleaching to look like the lighter-skinned woman). Ranks continued his narrative by denouncing the practice of bleaching and uplifting a more Afrocentric notion of blackness:

> Come black girl because ah you win di race
> Look how you cute and with you beautiful face . . .
> Ah true you nuh bleach dat is no disgrace . . .
> Tell dem black girl dat ah you win di race . . .
>
> (Come black girl because you have won the race
> Look at how cute you are with your beautiful face . . .
> It is true that you don't bleach and that is no disgrace . . .
> Tell them black girl that it is you who have won the race . . .)

When dancehall adherents from the inner cities and lower classes use dangerous and often forbidden dermatological agents to lighten their skin colours, they are often chastised and berated in the wider Jamaican community. Paradoxically, the class-biased dialogue is resoundingly quiet about the practice by upper- and middle-class individuals of visiting their dermatologists and obtaining medically approved skin lighteners. Christopher Charles discovered in his psychological study of the relationship between skin colour and identity in dancehall culture "the majority of skin bleachers do not suffer from low self-esteem", but "have incorporated a browning identity in their black self-concept to meet the external beauty requirements of the Eurocentric color code and their internal needs for social acceptance and social visibility".[15] This was pointed to in Miller's 1970s study where Jamaican adolescents from various colour groups exhibited a preference for clear skin because satisfaction with their body image was based on its close approximation to the Caucasian ideal.[16] Miller speculated that the male and female adolescents in his survey learnt their colour-coded notion of beauty from a mechanism that associates a certain colour type in the society with wealth, authority, social status and education.[17]

Indeed, these bleachers do participate in affirming a positive Afrocentric identity of blackness and black pride in the space of the dancehall and at the dancehall event because the dancehall is a predominantly black and Afrocentric space. However, this seeming ambivalence to the acceptance of one's skin colour as a marker of self-esteem and true "black" identity arises from the necessary movement away from the dark-skinned base of colour-coded Jamaican society and towards the hegemonic standard of whiteness or lightness. Blackness as identity is inherent and immutable but skin colour can be shifted. Browning as skin colour and individual identity is undeniably linked to the continuum of black Jamaican identity, but it is grounded on the pervasive colour and class identity that bestows status and personhood on Jamaicans. Darker-skinned men and women from Jamaica's inner cities have been historically situated at the base of Jamaica's race/colour/class structure and have learnt the lessons of Jamaican society well. Their negotiations for social mobility and space will continue to be played out on their self-representative canvasses and narrated in their own popular space: dancehall culture.

Ritualizing Male Mobility

In contemporary Jamaica, it is clear that women have been more flexible and willing to manipulate the occupational opportunities that have been thrown up by the pattern of capitalist expansion in the postwar era. These choices and accessible avenues of social mobility may be more accessible to Jamaican women because of the operation of gendered structures of power in patriarchal Jamaica. Although masculine and feminine identities are oriented around clearly differentiated poles, masculinities are more carefully guarded and policed than femininities. In this environment, the black woman is able to move more freely than her male counterpart along the contemporary socioeconomic ladder by utilizing multi-gendered openings created in a free-market, capitalist society.[18] For example, female sexuality has remained a tradeable and saleable commodity over time. Even though male sexuality in Jamaica is also tradeable, as with the examples of the "rent-a-dread", gigolo, toy boy and other types of male prostitution, it does not enjoy the same degree of social acceptance (overtly or covertly) as does the trade of female sexuality. Gendered notions of masculinity and male power implicitly negate the social acceptance of men overtly trading their sexuality for financial gain. Therefore, even in the face of its very existence, social and sexual taboos in Jamaica still negate and deny any public recognition of trade in male sexuality in either homosexual or heterosexual liaisons,[19] as this economic reality tampers with the hegemonic and often unrealistic image of man as hunter and provider. Women are therefore placed in a position where they can and do reap significant economic benefits by using their sexuality. This trade operates on a continuum with the popular and erotic flaunt, flirt and promise that has become so popularized in the dancehall at one end, and outright prostitution at the other.

The term higgler or ICI signifies a dark-skinned, overweight or mampy-size Afro-Jamaican woman dressed in tight, revealing, garish costumes with both large amounts of gold jewellery and one of many elaborate hairstyles that negate the traditional conventions of Eurocentric beauty. This image of (un)femininity is often considered obscene, loud and vulgar by traditionalists, as most higglers/ICIs present themselves in a forceful and volcanic eruption of loud voices, demanding postures and crass statements that are considered "unladylike". Though some men utilize the ICI sector as a route to economic mobility, its overt feminization makes it a tenuous avenue of escape. The men who do engage in these trading activities are not, as a general rule, referred to as higglers or ICIs but are described as "businessmen" or simply as someone who "sells clothes, shoes and foreign things inna Arcade/downtown".

The demand for domestic help or assistance in the household is another employment option that has been fuelled by the increasing number of women who enter professional careers outside of the home. This rise in professional and working women creates more openings for domestics – housekeepers, babysitters, nannies, washers, cleaners and cooks, among others. In a rigidly gendered society such as Jamaica, these openings are inaccessible to men because they are identified as women's work. A Jamaican man would have to deny and suppress his masculinity if he wished to identify with these overtly feminine roles. In fact, even if a man became desperate enough to apply for any such domestic post, he would have to overcome the suspicion and ridicule of the prospective employers, as they too subscribe to the traditional definitions of masculinity and femininity. This scenario was graphically depicted in an October 1999 episode of the popular Jamaican soap opera *Royal Palm Estate* on CVM TV, a Jamaican television station, when the young man who applied for a domestic position (helper) at Royal Palm Estate was turned away by Miss Joyce, the woman in charge of hiring. He later disguised himself as a woman and was hired by Miss Joyce to perform these domestic duties.

In this heavily policed and tightly gendered order, these and other viable avenues of economic mobility are barricaded by the patriarchal structures that are fixed both inside and outside the minds of Jamaican men. As a result, many of these men who fail to achieve the hegemonic goals of Jamaican manhood revert to ritualistic responses that are more accessible. Here, notions of sexuality become very important to many Jamaican men, especially those at the lower socioeconomic levels who have limited access to other symbols of real power that identify masculine status. A real man is one who can act as traditional hunter and provider. He is able to access the symbols of masculinity, that is, wealth and power – money, brand-name clothing, flashy cars, beautiful women. For the man who cannot access these symbols, the domination of women and issues of sex and sexuality attain primacy in laying the foundation for the definition of his identity. It may be argued that this phenomenon is a throwback to the freelance stud of the colonial era. Research in the dancehall shows that the concept of a *wukka man* (worker man)[20] who have "nuff gyal inna bungle" (many girls in a bundle)[21] is one that is actively subscribed to by men who are precariously placed on the lowest ledge of the race/class/gender nexus. As the sociopolitical and economic tensions deepen in Jamaica, these groups of men and women have increasingly limited access to the traditional and emerging symbols of social mobility that denote high status and personhood. These include, but are not limited to, socioeconomic background, high levels of education, white-collar career and economic wealth. Some of these women trade meaningful monogamous relationships for polygamous liaisons with wealthy and powerful men. In an inner-city context, the man's power would be found in his economic and social status in his community. These men include, for example, the don, area leader, druggist[22] or dancehall deejay. Their power is not only economic, but also political and often extends to the legitimacy, respect, authority or fear which the particular man generates, enjoys or invokes in his community or the wider Jamaican society. However, in their quest for elevated status and masculine identity some of these men traverse the more easily available and patriarchally sanctioned routes over, above and through the female body and feminine sexuality. The dancehall's slack, vulgar and sexual narratives – what I call "punaany lyrics" – encode these ritualistic and often empty forms of identity negotiation.

Courting and Conquering the Punaany

In the male-dominated dancehall dis/place, this negotiation for elevated status and identity is translated into the lyrical and stylistic courtship, conquest and dominance of female sexuality, femininity and women. Arguably, this is an instance of patriarchy's operation at its elemental, basest and most sexual level, where the most extreme manifestations of this behaviour are often perceived as misogynistic.

In the dancehall dis/place, lyrics that seek to court and conquer the female abound in the punaany lyrics. "Punaany" is a Jamaican colloquialism for the female genitals, the vagina, and is popular in dancehall narratives. A host of synonyms also exist in the dancehall including the terms *glammity, punash, pum pum, punny, good hole, renkin meat, tight underneath, vaggi* and *ukubit*. At the level of courtship, the lovers of punaany extol its praises and, like Shabba Ranks in his song "Love Punaany Bad", document their undying adoration for the punaany while simultaneously advertising their own control and competence in "taking care of" the punaany: "Love punaany bad, love punaany bad, love punaany bad, / mi a punaany guineagog" (I love vagina very much, I love vagina very much, / I am a vagina master).

In a related vein, Lecturer's rapturous treatise "Punaany too Sweet" reminds the dancehall audience that "every woman have a right fi damn boasy, / cause dem have something wheh every man want it" (Every woman has a right to boast excessively, / because she has something that every man wants). At the other extreme, the conquerors wage a lyrical war against this manifestation of female, as Spragga Benz outlines in his song "Jack It Up", where he entreats men to "Cock it up, jack it up, dig out di red" (Lift it up, hoist it up, dig out the red[ness]) and to "ram it and jam it and rev out di hole". "Di red", which is literally translated as "the red", refers explicitly to the moist, red labia of the vagina. In the dancehall, this also refers to the very essence of what is considered feminine and woman. The redness of the labia denotes a healthy, strong vagina and, by extension, a healthy, strong, aggressive woman whose submission or subjugation is symbolized by the forceful, painful removal and negation of the healthy red of the labia. Hence, Spragga Benz's exhortation to "dig out di red".

In a related discourse, Red Dragon's "Agony" outlines that he will not run away from any sexual challenge because, as he states, "Mi have di agony, man mi have di agony, / mi have di agony girls dem remedy" (I have the agony, oh yes I have the agony, / I have the agony, the cure for the girls/women).[23] For Red Dragon, he will successfully ride and ultimately conquer any manifestation of the punaany whether the woman is "big like ah elephant" or "mawga and cranky".

Shabba Ranks's reminder that "ooman caan dun" (woman can't done), in his song "Caan Dun", speaks to the dangers that the male courtier and conqueror face from the inimitable punaany. Shabba warns that the punaany "mek outa footbottom material and it caan rub dung" (is made from the same material as foot soles and cannot be worn down) while "man gone ah Mr Wong cause him body bruk dung" (men have to go to Mr Wong [for aphrodisiacs] because his body has broken down). Shabba's repeated warning to men against the punaany and its durability is a two-edged sword in the discourse of courtship and conquest. "Ooman caan dun but man body run dung" signifies the admirable power of women in the guise of the punaany as well as the sinister potential of this female power to decimate the male physique and his masculine essence.

This focus on the punaany was manifested in August 1988 at the second staging of Dancehall Night under the auspices of the then premier reggae show, Reggae Sunsplash, held at the Bob Marley Performing Centre in Montego Bay, Jamaica. Dancehall artistes were lyrically engaged in either courting or derogating femininity. The punaany took centre stage as these lyrics reached a deafening crescendo. The dancehall dalliance with lewd and slack lyrics extolling the virtues or negatives of female sexuality during the previous year,[24] had been honed and perfected through 1988. Encouraged by the interactive response and support of dancehall affectees, both in sales and accolades at dancehall events, both male and female deejays at Reggae Sunsplash 1988 were guilty of singing praises or savagely criticizing the size, shape and colour of the female anatomy. Though some members of Jamaica's traditional elite would express horror at the dancehall's "attack on the punaany" at the Bob Marley Performance Centre that Thursday night into Friday morning,[25] the dancehall audience felt no such dismay. The lyrical praises to and ritualistic treatises about the punaany all found favour among the men and women in the huge crowd that was estimated to be about fifty-six thousand at half-past-one in the morning, the peak time of the concert.

The male courtier or conqueror is frenetically concerned with subduing the punaany by any means and at all costs. It must be conquered before it becomes too powerful and results in the subjugation and submission of men and the corruption or elimination of their masculinity. In this instance, the punaany as the fleshly incarnation of the feminine other becomes a trophy whose conquest bequeaths an overtly masculine identity to the marginalized male.

This concern with the female sex organ, feminine sexuality and the female body as legitimate sites for male identity negotiation remains in popular dancehall culture. It has been matched and countered by the rise of the raunchy female artiste, heralded by the long reign of the Queen of Slackness, Lady Saw. These female artistes will either aggressively and demandingly ride the sexual thrust with their own suggestive and raw lyrics and performance, like Lady Saw, or rebuff the attacks on the female body and feminine sexuality with lyrics that derogate male sexual performance, courtship or conquest, like Tanya Stephens and Ce'cile.

Tanya Stephens's release of the dismissive "Yuh Nuh Ready fi Dis Yet" in 1996 pushed at the gendered boundaries of dancehall discourse when she lyrically berated the self-praising man for his lack of sexual prowess and his inability to truly satisfy women. Her chorus, "Yuh nuh ready fi dis yet, bwoy" (You are not yet ready for this, boy) rescripted the notion of male (sexual) superiority that is an important element of the sexual narratives of male dancehall artistes. Tanya's usage of the infantilizing term *bwoy* disses and denigrates the manliness that is encoded in the adult posture, profile and performance of the male's sexualized lyrics. Many of my own male interviewees at that time felt disrespected by the lyrics of the song and felt that Tanya was too aggressive, uppity and rude. In fact, one incensed male interviewee told me that Tanya needed a "good backshot inna har belly fi keep har quiet" (a good backshot up inside of her abdomen to keep her quiet/calm).[26] For men such as my respondent, women like Tanya upset the traditional patriarchal structure of masculine dialogue into which the dancehall courtier or conqueror plays.

In her 2003 song "Do It to Me Baby", Ce'cile discussed the practice of *bowing* and stated that she "love di man dem wheh dweet" (loves the men who do it). Her breathless exhortation "do it to me baby", a request to her man to perform cunnilingus, met resistance. In the dancehall, the word *bow* signifies the low status assigned to the concept where one must stoop down low to show deference or respect for a higher authority figure, in effect accepting one's own subservience and subjugation. Shabba Rank's "Dem Bow" highlighted the varying methods by which one identified the *bow cat,* including "man unda table"; "gyal a clean rifle"; "back teeth lik out"; and "lipstick pon hood head". For Shabba a bow cat is defined as either "a gyal weh suck off man cock" or as a man "wheh put him head unda frock". Both fellatio and cunnilingus are negated in this early dancehall treatise. However, the later exhortation by Baby Cham in his song "Boom" that his woman has to suck, that is, perform fellatio, shows the creeping tolerance in the dis/place for the practice of fellatio, as Baby Cham documents his own extreme ecstasy and the fact that his "yeye dem tun ova" when him "gyal a clean". Yet while there is now some evidence that fellatio may be an acceptable practice, because men are on the receiving end, nowhere in dancehall discourse has there been any treatise by a male artiste that encourages or supports cunnilingus.

In August 2003, I was part of a television interview panel on Cliff Hughes's *Impact* programme with Ce'cile and veteran dancehall deejay Ninjaman. During the interview, Ninjaman admonished Ce'cile for doing this song, which he felt was her own way of trying to encourage "di man dem fi start do dis ting" because these were the kind of practices or what he called "carelessness" that led to the demise of Sodom and Gomorrah. Ce'cile stated that disc jockeys refused to play the song on air, even though it used double entendre to discuss the practice. She also noted that Baby Cham's "Boom" was given significant airplay and a similar song by Beenie Man that encouraged women to perform oral sex was being played on air at that time. Dancehall men are unequivocal about the fact that they do not bow, and for Ce'cile, a dancehall artiste, to suggest that her male partner "bow to her" tampers with the sexual rituals that are idealized in the dancehall.

The Babyfather

The role of *babyfather* is another viable, socially sanctioned and sexual route to masculinity in Jamaica. A babyfather is a man who fathers an illegitimate child or several children. Each child serves as undisputed proof of his conquest of the punaany and the accompanying subjugation of the woman. The man who can become a babyfather multiple times over lays claim to high levels of masculine identity as a potent and virile man. Many men, particularly those from the inner city and lower and working classes are elevated and praised by their peers for siring multiple offspring. Those who do so with as many different mothers or who are "potent" enough to sire more than one child in the same year or month are elevated to the status of near myth or legend. They are "real" men. The paradox is that many show little or no concern about the economic and emotional welfare and upbringing of these children. Further, my research revealed that some of these babyfathers selected their potential babymothers with great care to ensure that these women were mature, responsible and financially secure enough to provide their children with a decent upbringing and a secure future in the inevitable absence of the man's support – economic, emotional, physical and otherwise.

The *champion jockey* is one example of sexual conquest as male empowerment at work in one inner-city community in Kingston, Jamaica that I will refer to as Waterhole. In Waterhole, *jockey* is a sexual play on the notion of riding and the concept is one of riding as many women as possible to become a champion. Many young men in communities like Waterhole become fathers at an early age because if they do not father children by the time they are around twenty-three years old, then their manhood becomes suspect and their peers will often cast derogatory slurs at them and chase them away from the "corner". In these communities, the corner acts as a strategic site of male socialization and male bonding, and access to it is treasured and protected.[27] At this particular corner in Waterhole a man does not become a man until he gets someone pregnant, and the concept of champion jockey as a status-generating tool is used to rank levels of masculinity among young men.

The year-long process or race culminates at the same time that traditional and uptown Jamaica engages in various New Year's Eve celebrations – New Year's Eve balls and parties, church vigils and watch nights, community vigils, family gatherings, and so on. At this time, groups of young and middle-aged men from Waterhole tally their list of conquests and the winner is crowned champion jockey for the year ended. Conquests must be more than casual dates, because the men have to prove that they have been involved in an intimate sexual relationship or liaison with their female conquests. A one-night stand cannot qualify as a new conquest, and the contestants for the supreme position of champion jockey must prove that they have had sexual relations with this woman several times, over an extended period of time. A pregnancy or birth of a child is the ultimate and most valuable proof of such relations. In an effort to ensure undeniable confirmation of these conquests, many of these men ensure that, during the course of the year, they conduct their liaisons and sexual activities openly. For example, inviting these women to their homes and publicly promoting their sexual trysts. Many prefer vigorous or violent sexual activities that elicit screams or moans from the woman and cause the tell-tale creaking or shifting of bedroom furniture that can be heard by neighbours or peeping Toms outside. Love bites (hickeys) can be strategically placed on conspicuous parts of the woman's body, such as the neck. All these actions help to ensure adequate confirmation of the couple's multiple sexual engagements.

Further, the man ensures that, where possible, he visits the woman's home and makes himself "man a yaad". Therefore, he would sleep over at her house and behave like the "man in residence". Where possible, he would also encourage his friends to telephone him at the woman's house while he is visiting. If either man or woman has an ongoing relationship with another partner, clandestine trysts are scheduled. Confrontations often develop, but these serve only to cement the man's position as conqueror. If the confrontation occurs between the two women, then the man in question is viewed as a sexual don, a virile man who has ultimate control over several women. If the confrontation occurs between two men, then the woman's main, legitimate partner reviles her as a loose woman or skettel. In some cases, the trespassing male abandons the cheating woman to the punishment meted out to her by her legitimate partner. In others, the legitimate partner dismisses the woman as damaged goods and discards her into the clutches of her new lover. In either scenario, the male ultimately gains ascendancy at the expense of the female.

On 31 December each year, these men gather on their corner and sum up their new conquests, as defined, for the year. Carryover conquests from the previous year do not qualify, neither can long-standing babymothers. Ultimately, the man with the most new conquests is symbolically crowned champion jockey and given the task of defending his title and, by extension, his ascension to the highest levels of public patriarchy in this narrow sphere. Defending his title for the succeeding year means the champion jockey must ride his way through as many sexual conquests as possible. Other contenders are mandated to "do better next year" and, therefore, would certainly undertake to engage in as many different sexual relationships as possible.

Many of the men who hang out at these corners are young (early teens to late twenties) and unemployed, underemployed or seasonally employed. Most are high-school dropouts with no marketable skills. Some are engaged in intermittent extra-legal or illegal activities as a means of earning an income. Others are supported by their mothers or babymothers/wives/spouses or by remittances from relatives in the diaspora, or what Barry Chevannes refers to as the "barrel connection".[28]

In the interlinked spaces of inner-city culture and the dancehall dis/place, the champion jockey is one expression of the interlinked and underlying processes at work in what dancehall culture identifies as the wukka man with "nuff gyal inna bungle" or the "Best Babyfather" and other such manifestations of extreme male sexuality activity, which is traded for higher levels of masculine status. Some men are able to maintain lengthy relationships based on both economic trade-offs and sexual liaisons with their multiple partners. Others, with little or no financial resources, also use the route of multiple sexual relationships to consistently symbolize and reinforce their masculinity. If this domination and control is based entirely on the private sex act, then it has to be publicly conducted. Therefore, each private sexual act or conquest is publicly parodied and declared by the male conqueror for confirmation. This public confirmation by his peers bestows higher levels of masculinity on the male conqueror.

Wife versus the Matie: Pitting Woman Against Woman

In the dancehall dis/place, "wife" refers to woman number one (that is, the man's current spouse or babymother). In very rare instances does it actually refer to a married woman. *Matie,* from the British colloquial use of "mate", refers to the sweetheart or "other woman" engaged in an extra-marital or extra-relationship affair with another woman's spouse. In the dancehall dis/place, the matie is cast in a negative light, a woman with a huge sexual appetite who lures men into relations, often against their will.

Using the opposing poles of wife versus matie, another popular route to male ascendancy and identity reinforcement in the dancehall dis/place is the pitting of woman against woman in a war for their men. In this war, the man often acts as instigator, referee and trophy. The ultimate outcome of this war is the crowning of man as king. In his 1994 song "Matie", Beenie Man negatively identifies the matie thus: "Matie ah nuh good sitten, / when matie pass all yuh mumma man missn" (Maties are not good things, / when a matie passes by even your mother's man goes missing).

The matie or "other woman" narrative in the dancehall during the early 1990s provided an arena for female-female contests for male trophies. Women were exhorted or entreated to vie with each other in a contest where the winner would be crowned the wife. Nonetheless, these treatises held out no real promise for a stable, monogamous relationship to the female combatants and the men often remained polygamous throughout. In this woman-versus-woman contest, the man ultimately remained the only true winner.

As a part of this discourse in the dancehall dis/place, women were encouraged to "maggle pon yuh mate". "Maggle pon yuh mate" literally translated means "model on your matie", that is, "show off, pose, posture or preen, when you see your man's other woman". This is exemplified in Cobra's exhortations to the masses of women who believe they are the wife as opposed to the matie in his song "Mate ah Rebel" when he states that

> Matie ah rebel but tell har go to hell
> Dis year mek she know ah di better hole tell . . .
> Matie nuh have no red left
> Har body done, yuh know
> Dat's why har man ah run come
>
> (Matie is rebelling against her fate but tell her to go to hell
> This year, let her know that the better hole will tell . . .
> Matie has no red left, her body is exhausted and sexually emptied
> That is why her man is now running to you)[29]

Spragga Benz expresses a similar sentiment in his own version of the matie treatise when he informs the wife that

Matie free paper bun
So get wile when yuh see har a come
Caw she yuh man trick, buy har a biskit den use har fi one night ah fun . . .
Matie body it dun but yuh know say you fresh an young . . .

(Matie's free paper has burnt – her time is up
So get wild when you see her coming
Because your man tricked her and bought her a biscuit and used her for
one night of fun . . .
Matie's body is done/finished, but you know that you are fresh and
young)[30]

In this case, woman number one, or the wife, would be the only woman who could legitimately "model" or "show off" to any other woman. Nevertheless, many convoluted linkages often develop in man-woman relationships and none of the women can lay claim to marriage and its ultimate prize, the man trophy. This makes the self-identification of oneself as wife or matie risky. Some women involved in these tangled relationships generally undertake a process of self-identification based on their perception of the level of care and attention they were receiving from the man in question (the trophy). The fact is, however, that the man trophy's inability, unwillingness or downright refusal to identify anyone as wife or matie (often plural wives and maties) would result in his retention of a consistent supply of willing women, eager to prove their worthiness for the coveted status of wife or woman number one. This process of negotiating the wife versus matie status was and still is, therefore, covertly and often overtly influenced and encouraged by many Jamaican men. Their ability to claim ownership of more than one willing and available woman as sexual partner, babymother or girlfriend gives these men the ammunition they need to symbolize and legitimize their identity as real men.

In popular dancehall culture, the matie phenomenon was, originally, linked only to intimate relationships between men and women. Once the term gained popularity and acceptance, it took on multiple meanings. For example, in the early 1990s in Jamaica, the *matie trample* was the name given to a particular type of women's shoes with thick, high heels. One could "trample down" (that is, step firmly and proudly upon and over) one's matie, both symbolically and realistically, if one acquired and wore shoes of this style. Many women became actively involved in "trampling down" their maties, real or perceived. Of course, the ICIs made significant profits from selling these shoes.

Around this same time, the *matie bag,* a miniature of the traditional knapsack, worn as a purse or pocketbook, also became popular among women. Matie clothes of various descriptions were available and the *matie frock* was especially popular at dancehall events. A matie hair-style was a cheap attempt to style one's hair into two ponytails to be worn at dancehall events where gaudy and expensive hairstyles were the rage. The *matie clip,* a direct result of the influx of mass-produced goods from the United States, was a cheap hair bow or clip, available at low cost and used in multiples to adorn the hair. Matie, therefore, meant cheap, less than and commonly available. The men were, however, noticeably absent from any active participation in this feminine arena and there were no masculine symbols of matie status. This ensured that men remained dominant at all times, acting as trophies and encouraging, entreating and exhorting the women in their struggles for ascendancy over each other. The popularity of these lyrical treatises in this era were symbolized by the ranking of Beenie Man's "Matie" as the third most poular song of 1994 and Cobra's "Done Wife" took the same spot for 1995.[31]

However, the subtle transformation from matie to skettel in the latter part of the 1990s was reflected in and influenced by transformations in the role and status of many Jamaican women. Even though some women were still dependent on men for favours, many others were becoming less financially dependent as they continued to access the escape routes provided by the increased impact of global capitalism on the Jamaican economy. In the dancehall dis/place, the independent ooman was less inclined to engage in verbal or physical contestations for wife status. Many such women could easily decide to accept matie status on the one hand, or become the "owna fi di man" on the other. Literally translated, "owna fi di man" means "the man's owner". As women, including many from a downtown, inner-city or lower-working-class background, accessed wealth through their entrepreneurial and other enterprises, many became able to "own a man" because they could provide him with resources like a car, expensive clothing, jewellery and gifts. This relationship was, therefore, based on the principle of exchange and these women called the shots. In many of these toy-boy liaisons, the women were usually much older than their teenaged or very young men.

Some women began to refer to each other affectionately as matie. "Wha'pn mi matie?" (What's happening my matie?) or "See mi matie ova deso" (See, my matie is over there) or "Me a har mate" (I am having a relationship with her spouse). The contestations of wife versus matie or matie versus matie were, therefore, transformed into contests of woman versus skettel.

The wife versus skettel syndrome in the dancehall dis/place parallels the whore versus Madonna syndrome where women are subtly encouraged by traditional, patriarchal mores to identify with the deified and idolized Madonna or wife, seen as the epitome of feminine beauty, attitudes and behaviour by men. Further, as with the Madonna/whore syndrome, the engagement which results in the labelling of a woman as whore or skettel is essentially beneficial to the man, since he is provided with easily accessible sexual subjects and opportunities to reinforce his sexuality and identity. Indeed, many women participate in this process. For example, the wife or woman is confident that her man's or husband's trysts with a skettel cannot tamper with the superordinate relationship she shares with him. This is because, in her estimation, a skettel is less than a wife or woman and cannot be elevated to higher status. The subjective and convoluted reasoning that underlies these gendered conclusions supports these relationships and ensures the continued superiority and domination of many men over their women, even with the rise of the independent ooman.

Like the super-wife cum career woman of traditional patriarchy, the idealized notion of "woman" fits flexibly into multiple markers of identification that highlight this deified status. For example, in popular dancehall culture, and, by extension, inner-city culture, the wife/woman is one who exhibits many of the following characteristics:

1. works hard;
2. "can read or have education" (is literate and educated up to or beyond the secondary level);

3. independent and able to take care of herself, her offspring and oftentimes her man, without his financial assistance;
4. "kip ongle one man" (has only one male sexual partner);
5. "have good hole" (possesses a tight, clean and well-cared for vagina that can purportedly satisfy her single male partner);
6. "nuh dash wey belly" (does not believe in or practise abortions);
7. "nuh haffi raffle har belly" (is clearly able to identify the father of her child and does not have to name multiple fathers-to-be upon pregnancy);
8. look good (is well proportioned and has a good body, as defined in the dancehall dis/place);
9. "have a cute face" (is beautiful or pleasing to the eye);
10. "smell good" (does not have offensive body or vaginal odours);
11. "dress good" (can afford expensive, brand-name clothing or expensive, locally made costumes and attends dancehall sessions in trendy regalia; dressing "good" also means that one wears flattering, sexy and revealing clothes but is not engaged in overt displays of sexuality in the dancehall event).

These factors provide a template that can be used to identify the wife/woman and to place her among the upper ranks of the female-female hierarchy in the dancehall dis/place.

In contrast, the term "skettel" is rooted in the most negative sites of feminine derogation. This type of woman is located at the base of the female-female hierarchy, even below the offending matie. Literally defined, the skettel is a "woman with loose morals who is easily available for sex". Other markers of skettel status are many, the majority of which are the direct opposites of the signifiers of wife/woman. For example, the skettel is defined as a woman who

1. is lazy and does not want to work;
2. "cyaan read an nuh have nuh sense or education" (is illiterate, stupid and ill-educated);
3. is dependent, often "kotching" with a friend, parents or an unwilling male partner and heavily dependent on others, including men, for financial support and sustenance;
4. "tek nuff man" (has multiple sexual partners, is promiscuous

[bordering on nymphomania] and easily available to any and every man);

5. has a "loose hole" (a vagina that had lost its elasticity and cannot provide her male partner any real sexual pleasure);
6. is a "cemetery" (a woman who has had one or more abortion);
7. "gi man jacket or raffle belly" (names the wrong man as father of her child or names multiple fathers-to-be upon pregnancy);
8. "nuh have no shape" (is not well-proportioned, as defined in the dancehall dis/place);
9. is ugly;
10. has offensive body and vaginal odours;
11. "cyaan dress" (wears ill-fitting or out-of-style costumes and often wears the same costume on multiple occasions); and
12. engages in overt displays of sex and sexuality in the dancehall event, specifically designed to lure unwilling and weak men into sexual liaisons.

The wife/woman versus skettel engagement and contestation continues to play itself out in the dancehall dis/place and among dancehall adherents in the wider society, as men and women actively engage in the identification and labelling of other women as skettels. However, like its predecessor, the matie, the skettel has also undergone some transformation. Its negative and debased meaning, has, over time, been distilled. For example, the term "skets", a diminutive and affectionate form of skettel, is sometimes used by women to refer affectionately to each other "Whap'n skets, how tings?" (What's happening skets, how are things with you?) or to identify themselves. During my own research in the dancehall, some women felt that the skettel had more flexibility, freedom and fun, and was able to choose for herself without excessive male interference or dominance. These choices range from sexual partners to lifestyles, career paths, clothing and entertainment, among others.

Further, while men engage in loud, vocal denunciation and derogation of skettels, their evidenced preference for these same women seems hypocritical. One young man from uptown (that is, Jamaican middle class) noted that he enjoyed being with skettels. He identified them as downtown (that is, Jamaican lower class) women from the ghetto who did not give a lot of problems. The fact that they loved parties, sex, hype clothes and were always ready and available to go out was appealing. Further, while these women loved money, he noted that they were still willing to work things out if you had none. Indeed, he felt that skettels were less demanding than the women from the middle classes and did not expect their men to behave nice and sweet. He was, of course, particularly taken with the sexual prowess of these skettels.

At this juncture, the skettel is the other woman in the Madonna/ whore binary that ultimately benefits men at the expense of feminine contestation. Here, skettel is defined by men and activated and legitimized by men. Women who actively choose to become skettels, or willingly subscribe to skettel-like behaviour, tamper with this opposition and destabilize the site of masculine identification and legitimacy.

Hidden Queens in the Dancehall

Indeed, for the woman in the dancehall dis/place, the knowledge of her power and value to the male as woman becomes a route to her ascendancy. If male heterosexuality is a valuable route to masculine identity, then her role as chief facilitator in this process can be used to ensure her access to resources. This ideology of male identification through sexuality in the dancehall is therefore utilized by their women in an erotically charged atmosphere of flaunt, flirt, promise and sometimes delivery. The queens of the dancehall, at all levels of the hierarchy, utilize their sexuality ruthlessly, from the lyrical mistresses like the raunchy Lady Saw and Tanya Stephens, to the queens of display epitomized by Carlene the Dancehall Queen, female modellers like the Ouch Crew and skilled dancers like Keiva, Stacey and Mad Michelle. As discussed later in this chapter, this trade-off is based on the ultimate positioning of man as chief gazer and prime resource giver. Where the role of women in the dancehall dis/place is concerned, it is noteworthy that the persona of dancehall queen; dancehall model or dancer is not homogeneous and neither is that of the raunchy deejay Lady Saw. Therefore, generalizations around these popular examples are risky.

In the dancehall, a large number of prominent queens exist, while others are regularly crowned and dethroned. These queens of the dancehall dis/place are neither as well known nor as legitimized in the broader Jamaican society as Carlene or the popular female deejays, like Lady Saw. Neither do they use overt displays of sexuality as their primary means of empowerment and identity. These queens fit more squarely in the category of independent ooman outlined in chapter 2 and discussed earlier. They are self-employed women who have gained some personal wealth and visibility through their own efforts and endeavours in the informal sector. They are daring, aggressive, loud and expressive, and wear expensive brand-name clothing that flaunts their voluptuousness and wealth. These "hidden" queens of the dancehall also wear elaborate hairstyles and engage in conspicuous consumption of expensive liquor at dancehall events. Most of these women are in a dominant economic position that allows them to choose the type of man they want to have intimate relations with, and many prefer younger men.

One important example of this high-status queen of the dancehall (exemplified in the identity group of independent ooman) is Sandra Lee. Sandra Lee is a part of the renowned ICI Lee clan that includes her mother, Mumma Lee, and her brother, Kaka Lee. They are established Arcade[32] higglers who, since the early 1980s, hold high status among the ICI fraternity in Jamaica. At the time of this research, Sandra Lee was the patron of a cosmetology salon in Half Way Tree, which she subsequently moved to downtown Kingston. She lays claim to a legacy of inner-city/downtown Kingston background and ICI/dancehall heritage that place her in a position of royalty in the dancehall dis/place. Sandra Lee is a regular dancehall patron and attends nearly all events hosted by the immortal dancehall sound Stone Love. Her arrival at any dancehall event, major, minor or otherwise, is heralded by an announcement over the sound system. For the duration of the event, her status in the dancehall is constantly reinforced by intermittent announcements over the sound systems of her presence and her continuous "featuring"[33] by the videographers and the display of her image on the closed-circuit television at the venue. This featuring ensures her presentation and re-presentation on the television monitors at the live event as well as on the videocassettes which will be duplicated and sold to dancehall adherents at home and in the diaspora. The video is also often featured on the

Sandra Lee in a regal pose at the Black & White Party at La Roose, Portmore, St Catherine, December 2000. Courtesy of Sandra Lee.

many local cable channels. The high level of respect that Sandra Lee commands in the dancehall dis/place is such that her persona and reputation are defended, violently or otherwise, by her supporters.

Christine Hewitt is another popular independent ooman in Jamaica. Her activities cut squarely across the multiple terrains of the ICI, traditional media, dancehall and uptown arts sectors. Her daring and radical personality is energized by her multiple roles as an ICI; music promoter and producer; former prime-time talk-show host on TVJ; host of her own talk programme on one of Kingston's local cable television channels; MC and promoter of dancehall and other cultural events; performer and poet. She is also featured in several music videos with prominent dancehall artistes, including Lady Saw. In late December 2004, Christine married a twenty-three-year-old man, eighteen years her junior.[34]

Other popular and prominent women in the dancehall dis/place at the time of the original research for this work included the Bashment Babes, models and dancers out of Montego Bay; the Ouch Crew; and the Hard Core Models. Since 2003, popular dancers Stacey, Keiva and Mad Michelle have also earned high status in the dancehall. Winners of the annual Dancehall Queen contest held in Montego Bay since 1997 also attain primacy and publicity in the dancehall dis/place in Jamaica as well as in the diaspora. However, veterans Carlene, the Dancehall Queen, and Lady Saw, the Queen of Slackness, still remain two of the most prominent and public faces of women in the dancehall.

Carlene. the (Facilitated) Browning Queen, Lady Saw, the (Negated) Slack, Black Queen

I argue that Dancehall Queen Carlene's meteoric rise to popularity both within and beyond the dancehall was facilitated by the intersection of the race/class/colour distinctions that maintain a sociopolitical hierarchy within Jamaican society. Carlene is a Jamaican browning. As argued earlier, the historical legacies of slavery and colonialism have ensured that Jamaican society remains highly colour-biased. Women with skin colouring and other phenotypical features that closely approximate a European ideal are favoured over others whose skin colour and facial features do not. In the dancehall dis/place, this places Carlene in a privileged position over other women of a darker hue.

In addition, while she originally socialized and conducted her activities mainly within the dancehall dis/place, Carlene could not claim true inner-city or lower-class status, as her background is lower middle class. Further, Carlene has a secondary education and is able to display and deliver herself in public, in the media and other social settings of the middle- and upper-class variety in a fashion and with mannerisms that approximate the standards of "decent" behaviour set by traditional Jamaican society. Carlene's grasp and use of the preferred standard English in public spaces like the media and social settings which demand this flexibility also affords her more social legitimacy over other women who are either unable or unwilling to converse in standard English and who resort to the use of vernacular. The publicly soft-spoken Carlene is therefore able to pass easily between the boundaries of upper-middle- and upper-class society in Jamaica since her background, education, mannerisms and skin colour make her an ideal candidate for such status.

The traditional Jamaican attitude to a browning such as Carlene, who engages in what is perceived as deviant behaviour in the dancehall, is almost like that of a doting parent with a naughty child: a little slap, some half-hearted scolding. This is underscored by a high level of tolerance and full confidence in that child's ability to rise above such petty behaviour, since he or she has benefited from socialization and exposure at a higher and more accepted level. Carlene's public sexual posturings and gyrations are tolerated and subtly encouraged by traditional society. This attitude opened the way for the use of Carlene's scantily clad image as the advertising icon for the Slam Condom line. The perception also figured prominently in the selection of Carlene as the representative of Courts Jamaica Limited (a furniture and appliance chain) in its advertising campaigns in 1998 (along with scantily clad dancers) and 1999 (along with deejay Beenie Man), and it has also facilitated Carlene's transition from dancehall queen to co-host of *Our Voices,* a television programme that she initially hosted with Lisa Hanna, Miss World 1993. *Our Voices* is now aired on Monday nights on CVM Television.

In the dancehall dis/place, however, many affectors and affectees are fully aware of Carlene's facilitated status but feel compelled to credit her for exposing and promoting a facet of dancehall culture, as one dancehall videographer noted:

You know that Carlene is one of the women right now who cause people to ensure that they look good because when they see you . . . because, alright now, do you know that there are many girls . . . a lot of girls out there that look better than Carlene. A lot of girls but they are not being pushed up (promoted) like Carlene you know . . . A whole heap of girls are out there, okay? But we have to give her (Carlene) her credit because she . . . made this thing what it is you know.[35]

Carlene remains the de facto dancehall queen to this day. On the other hand, Lady Saw is a Jamaican woman of dark skin colour and a working-class background. Her long-term career and ascendancy to the highest levels of the deejay fraternity have been consistently marked by intense and harsh criticism from traditional Jamaica.

Lady Saw's constant output of sexually explicit lyrics has resulted in her being crowned the Queen of Slackness and attracting negative publicity. Unlike her sexually explicit and hedonistic model/dancer counterpart, Carlene, deejay Lady Saw has been subjected to more negative than positive publicity. This is based on the perceptions of her "vulgar" and slack role in the dancehall dis/place by members of the broader Jamaican society. Although her ascendancy to the throne of slackness was heavily critiqued and publicized, this has served to cement her position as the lyrical queen of slackness in the dancehall dis/place. Lady Saw has constantly noted in her interviews that her early dalliance with cultural and conservative lyrics resulted in little response, if any, from the adherents of the dancehall. Therefore, her transition to sexually explicit lyrics and suggestive performative style was more of an economic than an ideological decision. This prompted her to pen her scathing institutional critique in the song "Slackness", which was released on her 1996 album *Give Me the Reason*. "Slackness" attacked the institutional hypocrisy and pointed critics and traditionalists away from critiques of her dalliance with sex and sexuality and towards more pressing issues in the society:

> Society a blame Lady Saw fi di system dem create
> When culture did a chat dem neva let me through di gate
> Now as mi say "sex" dem waan fi jump pon mi case
> Slackness is when di road wan fi fix

Slackness is when govament break dem promise
Slackness is when politician issue out gun
So di two party ah shot dem one anedda dung

(Society is blaming Lady Saw for the system that they created
When I used to sing cultural lyrics I did not get any publicity [or money]
Now, as soon as I say "sex" they want to say all kinds of things about me
Slackness is when the roads need repairing
Slackness is when the government breaks its promises
Slackness is when politicians issue/distribute guns
So that the members of the two political parties can shoot each other
down)

In the face of her overwhelming popularity as the undisputed queen of slackness in the dancehall dis/place, Lady Saw has, over time, become more accepted and tolerated by the wider society as one of those "negative and deviant elements" in the dancehall dis/place. Yet she does not enjoy the level of acceptance, legitimacy and pampering from the wider society as does Carlene, the Dancehall Queen, nor has her image or voice been used in any advertising campaign in Jamaica. Lady Saw's dark skin colour and her claim to a poor, grassroots background (from the rural parish of her birth in St Mary to her thrust for stardom in the dis/places of Kingston) places her at the lowest point of the race/class/ colour hierarchy of traditional Jamaican womanhood. Therefore, while more focus is placed on her role as a disseminator of sexually explicit lyrics, the underlying ideological contestations and hidden dialogue are actually focused on her identity as a lower-class, black-skinned, country girl who seeks to re-present herself in the urban public spaces of Jamaican media and dancehall performance. In addition, Lady Saw operates in the dancehall dis/place in a role and space that has been defined as overtly masculine – using sexually explicit lyrics. Here, one again finds historical issues of race/class/colour coming to bear on what is accepted and legitimated and what is tolerated or not in the wider terrain of gendered practice and behaviour in Jamaica.

Sexual Liberation of Women in the Dancehall

As outlined earlier, heterogeneous images of femininity exist in the dancehall dis/place. I have assigned different labels that reflect the activities, world view and perception of these re-presentations of femininity in the dancehall dis/place. These images have been identified and categorized based on certain criteria – age, socioeconomic background, education, number of children, career type, among others – and include Miss Hotty Hotty, bashment girl, independent ooman/big ooman and skettel.

The image of dancehall model or dancer that has been associated with Carlene, the Dancehall Queen has become popularly promoted as a homogeneous site of liberation for female sexuality in the dancehall. Yet, based on my own longstanding work and immersion in the dancehall I find it prudent to underline the fact that while this heterogeneous image of femininity may be engaged in what could be classified as liberatory sexuality, this feminine persona is more so actively engaged in the promotion of a capitalist-influenced sexuality for the benefit of men. This engagement is essentially an economic trade-off where the sexiest, most flexible and *phattest*[36] dancehall model or dancer receives economic rewards in various forms, including trophies, cash and trips abroad. Other rewards might include features in such media as dancehall music videos on national or international television, local videos of dancehall events produced by dancehall videographers, popular dancehall newspapers or magazines,[37] photographs on dancehall posters for upcoming events and photographs on posters as performers or stars at upcoming events.

Over time, some popular contests among women in the dancehall dis/place have been used to crown or dethrone popular images of sexually explicit femininity. For example, following the 1997 release and success of the Island Jamaica film *Dancehall Queen,* an annual Miss Dancehall Queen contest has been held in Montego Bay. Contestants come not only from Jamaica, but also from the rest of the world. The elimination and finals are conducted in one night, with emphasis being placed on the voluptuousness, sexuality, display and dance prowess of the contestants. The winner must, for the benefit of the judges and audience, demonstrate an overtly sexual aura in her dress as well as stage presence and dancing style. The winner of this contest enjoys a one-year reign, similar to that of the Miss Jamaica (World or Universe), complete with trips abroad and a ceremonial handing over to her successor the following year. This is a coveted title in the dancehall dis/place, as the winner of the annual Dancehall Queen contest gets the opportunity to travel abroad extensively and is featured prominently in videos of key dancehall events in both Jamaica and the diaspora as well as in the music videos of popular dancehall artistes. The 2002 Dancehall Queen contest was won by a Japanese woman, Junko Kudo, who subsequently gained tremendous popularity in the dancehall dis/place. Junko's crowning signalled dancehall's ability to cross racial, ethnic and geographical barriers and to incorporate diverse elements into its informal space.

Another similar contest was the Miss Buff Bay/Miss Buffer Zone contest popularized by the then Cactus Nightclub in Portmore, St Catherine and often featured in the popular dancehall-influenced newspapers of the time. Women who are phat (specifically, women who possess large or protruding labia) were encouraged to display this special endowment in the *HardCopy* newspaper or to enter the contest whenever it was held at the Cactus Nightclub or elsewhere. The "Buffer Zone" is also, at times, referred to as "Buff Bay" in dancehall slang. During this contest, judges would often check for authenticity to see if the labial protrusions were real, because women in the dancehall have been renowned for using artificial aids like sanitary napkins to enhance their phatness as part of their dancehall costuming. Women used these artificial aids to enhance their "buff" and, by extension their sexuality, for the benefit of the male gaze. Consequently, in an effort to prove their authentic claims to "buff status", women allowed the photographers and/or judges to palm their vaginas. During these competitive engagements, very little was left to chance and contestants were scantily clad in bikinis or G-strings. The more daring would give the judges and the audience a quick peek at the natural buff. During my own visits to two such contests, this sexual display provided a great deal of erotic stimulation to audience members, especially men.

One such Miss Cactus Buff Bay contest was held at the Cactus Nightclub in August 1998. The contest was held on a Thursday night, generally labelled "Girls Night Out". Contestants, who were clad in skimpy bikinis or lingerie, displayed their buff to the keen eyes of the male judges on the elevated stage and to the respectively admiring and lascivious glances of the female and male members of the "bashment" crowd. The women were encouraged to "skin out" and "go pon yuh head top" and engage in other gymnast-like antics to display their buff. Their overtly enthusiastic displays drew numerous shouts of praise from the male fans and encouraging screams and a few jealous sighs from the women in the audience.

That night, the prizes at stake were entirely financial: first prize of J$20,000, second prize of J$10,000 and third prize of J$5,000. To add to the hype and hilarity, one of the judges proceeded to "weigh" each contestant's buff with his hand, placing his hand between her legs and resting it, palm upwards, against her vagina. This was accompanied by the envious and supportive cries of the women and men in the audience.

The Treasure Chest competition was also associated with the Cactus Nightclub in Portmore, St Catherine, and enjoyed heavy coverage in the dancehall newspapers. The women who entered this contest were naturally endowed with large, full breasts. Contestants took part in a two- or three-round elimination process over two or three nights, much to the delight of the audience. This contest was, again, about much more than large, beautiful breasts, since the contestant with the largest breasts was never generally crowned the winner. The winner also had to have a sexy or "hot" body and had to be able to give adequate sexual displays of her body and her prized "Treasure Chest". These displays proved important in the selection of the winner and contestants were often ridiculed by the demanding audience, as noted in *HardCopy* on one such final:

> Next up was Kenisha who was sexy enough to give the other contestants a run for their money. She was followed by Shelly who had placed second in the previous week's elimination round. She showed off what she had to good measure, so much so that she almost suffered a spill as her ample bosom threatened to overflow her skimpy top. She was followed by the first round's second place winner and the biggest travesty of justice in the competition, Kerry Ann. If this competition was being judged solely on size, she would have won hands down. However, size isn't everything. Although she got a huge response from the crowd, it was hard to tell if they were cheering or laughing.[38]

A contestant poses at Cactus Nightclub in Portmore, St Catherine, March 1993. Courtesy of the Gleaner Company Limited.

At the finals of one such contest, the winner copped the Cactus Treasure Chest Trophy along with J$20,000. The first runner-up received a gift basket and J$10,000 and the second runner-up a gift basket and J$5,000. One other contestant also received a gift basket for her endearing and pleasant attitude.

Some other contests that exist(ed) in the dancehall dis/place include the Miss Healthy Body, Miss Impy Skimpy, Miss Stiff Breast, Miss Wet Breast, Miss Go-Go Wine and outright dance contests.[39] Many of these contests are now defunct. However, the creative dance hype of the dance-hall means that dance contests endure. The best dancer at a dancehall event is consistently featured on the now prominent videos produced by people like Jack Sowah of Sowah Productions. These women are solicited to attend prominent dancehall events and are at times paid an enter-tainer's fee to come and "vibes up di place".[40] It has become common practice for posters advertising future dancehall events to also advertise featured dancers and/or models as part of the hype associated with these events. Further, many of the videos that are made of these events are con-sumed internationally and some girls are "given a break" (that is, given access to resources and a chance at personal mobility) when they are invited on an all-expenses-paid trip to visit a fan abroad. This fan is usu-ally a man who has developed a particular fondness for that flexible and well-proportioned woman after watching her performance over time and wishes to meet her in person. Implicit in this exchange is the promise of sexual favours in return for the financial outlay (such as plane fare and other expenses) provided by the man. In one interview, Jack Sowah noted that

> Right now you have girls wheh deh a England an America true my videocassette. Racquel from Modelling Crew is in England an . . . Little Bit . . . she is also in England. Mackieboo, she's in England. Lisa is in . . . no . . . Mackie is in New York, Lisa is in England. An . . . couple a dem well yuh nuh leave here an go abroad true di video . . .

> (Right now there are girls [women] who are in England and America because of my videocassettes. Raquel from the Modelling Crew is in England . . . and Little Bit . . . she is also in England. Mackieboo, she is in England. Lisa is in . . . no . . . Mackie[boo] is in New York and Lisa is in England. Quite a few of them have left here and gone abroad because of the videos.)[41]

One should note that a trip abroad ("going to foreign") is a highly prized avenue of social and economic mobility for many Jamaican men and women, particularly those from the inner cities and the lower working classes. An opportunity to visit the United States, England or Canada is perceived as an instant marker of status and economic and social mobility.

Therefore, for women engaged in these contests and activities, the economic trade-off, which includes cash, trips abroad, appearances at dancehall events, trophies and so on, is well worth the overtly sexual displays. Many of these women prefer this avenue to that of labouring for minimum wages in the traditional employment sectors because their levels of education and training negate their abilities to access any positions that would attract significant remuneration. Since most come from poor rural or urban inner-city backgrounds, their chances at social mobility are further negatively affected. For many of these women their access to economic and other resources within this eroticized sector of the dancehall dis/place makes it a site of personal achievement, advancement, and social and economic mobility.

Women who enter the public zone of the dancehall as models, dancers or contestants possess not only the requisite physical attributes, but also embody a sense of the power of their femininity. Further, they are imbued with high levels of daring that negate any traditional norms of decent, feminine behaviour. This aggressive attitude does signify a departure from the traditionally accepted and constrained mores of decent feminine behaviour that exist in Jamaica, yet at first glance this attitude has often been read as a total erosion of the traditional male/female boundaries. It is true that the daring fashions and erotic display which accompany these particular women's prowess on the dancehall stage are overtly threatening to traditional Jamaica. Their activities, behaviours and costuming tamper with the normative expectations of how the female body should be clothed or exposed or positioned and how it should move in a public space. These women act as a radical and threatening counter-narrative to the expectations that form the master-narratives of traditional Jamaica.[42]

Yet while these erotic displays of female sexuality project a subversive narrative, the embodiment of these dancehall models, dancers and queens remains locked within the boundaries of patriarchy. The attention, rewards and accolades given by admiring men to holders of a prizewinning buff serve to legitimize and perpetuate these women's willingness to engage in overtly sexual displays of their vaginas in return for the attention or rewards generated. The sexual displays and suggestive gyrations of the dancehall queens titillate male sexual fantasies and feed into male perceptions of women as sexual objects. Therefore, these displays cannot be classified as either female-female reinforcement or as female self-idolation in isolation. On the contrary, they are primarily direct female-male engagement and these women broker some level of advancement in their own self-empowerment as a kind of residual benefit, almost by default. Consequently, while there have been arguments for the sexual liberation and freedom of these women,[43] my own participant research as a woman in the inner spaces of the dancehall reveals that the sexual parade of a dancehall queen, model, dancer, Healthy Body, Buffer Zone or Treasure Chest is not homogeneous among women in the dancehall. Not all dancehall women wear erotic, revealing costumes or engage in sexual display and flaunt their bodies. Many women who are dancehall adherents fall into the less sexual and erotically charged categories of dancehall model or dancer or that of Miss Thing or Miss Vogue, while others exist on the fringes of the four categories of female affectees identified in chapter 2 and defy classification into any one group.

My research shows that, in most instances, the sexual display and erotic pose of these particular women are presented for the masculine gaze. There are instances where women do take pleasure in being the focus of the masculine gaze as they parade their flamboyant and revealing costumes across the dancehall space. Further, there are examples where women revel in homoerotic pleasure as women performing for women. Yet I argue that many of the economic and other rewards reaped by the women in the dancehall come directly from men in an exchange that serves to underpin and legitimize the sexual identity of men and their superior position over women. For example, the various contests are promoted, hosted and funded by men as part of their economic endeavours and promotion of their enterprises without any corresponding or similar contests of erotic display or dalliance featuring men in the dancehall dis/place.

These contests also provide a space for the contestation of sociopolitical values at work in Jamaica. They provide an arena for the sexual display of women from the marginalized dis/place who are unable to legitimately ascend to primacy in the plethora of contests that are carried out and legitimated in the wider Jamaican society. Arguably, the Miss Buff Bay, Miss Buffer Zone, Dancehall Queen, Dancehall Model, Miss Impy Skimpy, Miss Treasure Chest and similar types of competitions exist at one end of a continuum of female-female contests which essentially have the same goal – the sexual display of women in varying stages of (un)dress.

In traditional Jamaican society, there are several competitions among women that are legitimated, including Miss Jamaica World, the Miss Jamaica Universe, Miss Fashion Model, Supermodel of Jamaica, Miss Petite Fashion Model, Miss Festival Queen, Miss Independence, Miss Farm Queen and Miss Jamaica Teenager. An important role of these traditional contests is to uplift and legitimize the images of femininity that are placed higher on the race/class/colour continuum of Jamaican society. These images invariably show women of lighter skin colour whose features approximate more closely the Eurocentric ideal that is perceived as the standard for international beauty contests. Additionally, women who have attained higher levels of education and exposure have greater chances of winning or placing in the top five. The simultaneous operation of the race/class/colour variables denies dark-skinned women from lower-class backgrounds with limited education any real place in these contests. Therefore, contests that focus on erotic display, sexual dalliance and dance prowess in the dancehall dis/place, like Dancehall Queen, Miss Buffer Zone and Miss Stiff Breast, also serve to undermine the operation of inherent colour and class biases in the wider Jamaican society. Their presentation of black, lower-class and grassroots femininity and eroticism in a public arena gives legitimacy and a sense of personhood to a particular group of women. These women would otherwise have been denied the publicity and access to resources by the society in which they were formed and exist.

Therefore, arguments for the increased sexual freedom and independence of women cannot be generalized within this male-dominated, highly patriarchal dancehall dis/place. In chapter 2, I documented the identity of the independent ooman whose control of economic resources allows her personal and sexual freedoms and often aids her to become "di owna fi di man" in a relationship where she is the chief provider for and often much older than her male partner. I also acknowledge the utilization by dancehall queens, models and dancers of female sexuality in an engagement incorporating flaunt, flirt, promise and sometimes delivery in order to access economic resources from men in exchange for heightened levels of masculinity that are subsequently bestowed on these men. I must argue strongly, however, against any generalized labelling of dancehall as an arena that facilitates the sexual liberation of women based solely on its lyrical output. The dancehall is a black popular cultural site that is very patriarchal and heavily male dominated. Although popular women like Dancehall Queen Carlene, female artistes like Lady Saw, Tanya Stephens and Macka Diamond, and dancers such as Stacey and Keiva have gained prominence and economic and social power within its boundaries, the dancehall evolved as and remains a predominantly masculine space under masculine power and control. This is consistently evidenced by the high proportion of male artistes in relation to the limited number of female ones and the corresponding proportion of male versus female promoters, managers and producers in the dancehall. Since the beginning of the twenty-first century, there has been a steady increase in the number of female artistes. This group now includes the popular Ce'cile, Macka Diamond (formerly Lady Mackerel), Miss Thing, Sasha and Queen Paula, who follow in the footsteps of veteran deejay Lady Saw and other foundation artistes from the 1980s like Sister/Mumma Nancy, Shelly Thunder and Junie Ranks. The recent move into producing by veteran artistes Lady Saw and Lady G is linked to the rise of new technology and ease of access to their own studio facilities, on the one hand, and to the progressive loosening of the gendered strictures that encircled the production sector in Jamaican dancehall, on the other.

This loosening confirms that the dancehall dis/place exists within a historical space that encourages the widening or loosening of the traditional patriarchal boundaries and facilitates male and female renegotiation of the rigid traditional sociopolitical and socioeconomic roles as defined by traditional Jamaican society. Within this renegotiated space, there are strong patriarchal factors that seek to uplift and preserve the

DJ Macka Diamond (formerly Lady Mackerel) poses with Lady Saw (right) at Macka Diamond's birthday bash at Back Yaad, Kingston, January 2005. Courtesy of the Gleaner Company Limited.

masculine without any wholesale elimination of the traditional patriarchal boundaries in the dancehall dis/place. Within this space, male heterosexuality and polygamy are revered and treasured because they embody the productive core of masculine identity. On the other hand, male homosexuality is denounced because they embody its reductive seeds. The following discussion examines dancehall's perception of and responses to male homosexuality.

"All Battyman fi Ded!" Dancehall's Strident Renunciation of Male Homosexuality

In the dancehall dis/place, the use of sex and sexuality to reinforce and identify masculine identity is also reflected in an overt paranoia of male homosexuality and all it symbolizes.[44] Dancehall songs like Buju Banton's "Boom Bye Bye" and those in the late 1990s and beyond that fit into the *chi-chi man* genre[45] reaffirm the gendered notion that, based on their historical experience, many Jamaican men identify and negotiate their masculine identity status through their sexuality and their seeming dominance of and power over the Other, that is, woman. The cultural dialogue in the dancehall is grounded in an ideological stance that draws significantly on this gendered foundation, which is then married to other religious, moral and cultural imperatives in Jamaica and the region. Where dancehall narratives about male homosexuality are concerned, however, the focal point moves from the high end of the sexual continuum, where it projects narratives that legitimize male-female intimacy and sexual relationships, to its low end, where these narrative projections stridently negate male-male intimacy and sexual relationships.

In the sociocultural context of the dancehall, to be gendered female is to be dominated and powerless. Therefore, if a man engages in sexual activities with another man he becomes feminized and thereby loses masculine dominance and power. Further, to condone male homosexuality is to reveal an ideological overview that legitimizes and supports the feminizing and subsequent loss of power of men. On the other hand, to publicly take a violent, anti-homosexual stance is to express one's accordance for masculinity, male sexuality and male dominance even when this individual has no real intent or history of physical assault against gay men.[46]

Indeed, even when they are not practising Christians, dancehall affectors and affectees claim the strong fundamentalist Christian religious imperatives that underpin Jamaica as one important element in the constitution of their discomfort with male homosexuality. This includes scriptures like the aforementioned story of Sodom and Gomorrah in Genesis 19 and verses that condemn homosexuality like those in Leviticus 18:22, 20:13 and in the New Testament, Romans 1:26–27. The directive given to man and woman by God in the creation story in Genesis 1:28 is also important in dancehall culture. Dancehall artistes believe that man and woman are to "be fruitful and multiply" and, for them, this is why God created Adam and Eve, not "Adam and Steve".

Patrick D. Hopkins notes that the most obvious form of gender treachery "occurs as homosexuality, bisexuality, cross-dressing and feminist activism".[47] This means that the heterosexist notions and practices that support anti–male homosexual paranoia are interrelated with behaviours and practices that are labelled misogynistic. Indeed, they are two sides of the same anti-feminine discourse that police the boundaries of gendered codes and behaviours of masculinity in patriarchal societies like Jamaica. Consequently, the behaviours, practices and sexual preference of homosexual men in Jamaica splinter the accepted notions of self that underpin the lives of heterosexual men in a patriarchal society. Homosexuality is, therefore, viewed as a "threat to manhood (masculinity) and correspondingly . . . a threat to personhood (personal identity)".[48] My own research in dancehall culture[49] shows that homophobia in the dancehall dis/place is actually a radical and extreme manifestation of Jamaican masculine paranoia of the feminine, where male homosexuals are deemed gender traitors who violate the accepted rules of gender identity and gender performance. Here, the dancehall as inner-city culture and Jamaican popular culture actively and consistently articulates, re-presents and performs its own version of this masculinized discourse in the form of anti–male homosexual treatises. These anti-homosexual treatises are a part of the wider terrain of a patriarchal structure that works to empower the Jamaican male. Cecil Gutzmore notes that "the earliest directly homophobic reggae song . . . is the 1978 King Sounds and the Israelites' 'Spend One Night Inna Babylon' . . . which makes explicit mention of Sodom and Gomorrah and of the fact that these two ancient cities . . . are anathematized in the Bible".[50] The anti-feminine paranoia in Jamaican popular culture that seeks to police male heterosexuality is most exemplified in the rise in anti-gay discourses in dancehall culture since the late 1990s.

Accordingly, the current response of the greater majority of heterosexual Jamaican men to male homosexuality is somewhere on a continuum of mild unease and tolerance to raging paranoia. This is the kind of raging paranoia that met the August 1997 directive of then commissioner of corrections Colonel John Prescod to distribute condoms in prisons in an effort to stem the spread of HIV/AIDS. His directive was seen by some men as a public acknowledgement of the "hidden secret" of their homosexual activities in prison and the gross miscalculation of the high levels of anti-homosexual paranoia in the prison population resulted in the untimely murder of sixteen male prison inmates.

In his own work on male socialization in the Caribbean, Chevannes outlines the contradictory and ambivalent mix of community mores and practices that underscore male and female tensions with male homosexuality in Afro-Jamaican communities.[51] This ambivalence is replicated in the dancehall's treatment of male homosexuality. Popular artistes like Beenie Man, Buju Banton, Elephant Man and Vybz Cartel are the most visible portion of dancehall and represent an internationally popular cultural group that has been, by default, labelled "Jamaican ambassadors-at-large". These artistes and other dancehall affectors draw upon their own experiences as Jamaican men and the historical experience of Caribbean and Jamaican people to mimic anti-homosexual feelings in extreme, condemnatory performances using creative lyrics and slang. Without a doubt, these anti–male homosexual treatises are often extremely violent, crass and biased, but they follow dancehall's tendency to deal in hard truths and tear away the mask of hypocrisy that has cloaked the lives of homosexual men (and women) in Jamaica. At the same time, the international visibility of the dancehall as Jamaica's contemporary and popular music form has resulted in inevitable local versus global tensions and clashes about the violent content of these anti–male homosexual treatises. This local-global clash of gender, sexuality and popular culture that Buju Banton faced in the early 1990s[52] was revitalized with the international campaign in 2004 against the anti-homosexual lyrics of eight male dancehall artistes Beenie Man, Bounti Killa, Buju Banton, Capleton, Elephant Man, Sizzla, TOK and Vybz Cartel by gay rights groups led by the UK-based Outrage!.[53] This anti-dancehall campaign was fuelled by the vociferous and explicit nature of the anti-homosexual dialogue in the dancehall since the late 1990s.

My research shows that this rise in anti-homosexual dancehall lyrics is a direct result of the progressive unmasking of (male) homosexuality since the late 1990s. This has been reflected in growing numbers of openly homosexual men on television programmes broadcast during prime-time on cable television stations that are accessible to Jamaicans. These include *Will and Grace, Queer as Folk* and *Queer Eye for the Straight Guy.* Many popular sitcoms also broadcast episodes that feature actors as homosexual men and women. The formation of the Jamaica Federation of Lesbians, All-Sexuals and Gays (JFLAG) in December 1998 acted as another catalyst when it raised the visibility of proud, gay Jamaican men and women. Homosexuality in Jamaica has been tolerated for many decades, cloaked under a hypocritical kind of "respectable" silence as long as gays "do their thing" in private and accept ritualistic ridicule or culturally sanctioned abuse as a part of their routine marginalization.[54] Thus the response of upper- and middle-class Jamaica to the open panorama of homosexuality since the 1990s has generally been cloaked in this accepted respectable silence. On the other hand, the overtly paranoid response of hardcore dancehall affectors and affectees, many of whom hail from Kingston's inner cities, has been exemplified by the significant increase in anti-homosexual dancehall songs and lyrics. In its early years, dancehall lyrics mentioned gay men (or women) in a line or two of a song. By the end of the 1990s and into 2004, entire songs of the chi-chi man genre were devoted to condemning male homosexuality as a vile abomination that threatened to corrupt and overturn Jamaican society, like the Biblical example of Sodom and Gomorrah. Rastafari-influenced artistes such as Capleton were busy "bunning out the chi chi" that had blossomed across the topography of Jamaican sexuality.

Chevannes's work on male socialization and my own research in the terrain of dancehall culture show that men in the inner city and in the dancehall dis/place generally view lesbianism in a rather paternalistic manner.[55] The overarching narrative is that lesbianism is pseudo-sex between women but as soon as these women have sex with "a real man" (often identified as the respondent) they will recant their "evil" ways. Female homosexuality cannot undermine the traditional tenets of Jamaican patriarchy because, based on their lack of a real penis – a significant biological definer of masculinity – none of these actors can be socially elevated to true masculine status by the wider society. The dancehall, or inner-city male in particular, views lesbianism as a corruption of femininity that exists between or among females in a very feminine context. As a result, this man views female homosexuality as powerless and lacking any real ability to threaten or undermine hardcore masculine identity.

During my work in the dancehall, those individuals whose stated/perceived background or current socioeconomic status was either lower or working class were more aggressive and loud in their vocal denunciations of male homosexuals. Yet, they were unable to explain why they took this defensive and aggressive and often violent stance. Many of my interviewees resorted to quoting Biblical scriptures in order to support their attitudes. Nonetheless, it is clear that many men and women in Jamaica have internalized the extreme anti–male homosexual paranoia that pervades patriarchal societies. The cacophony of "Boom Bye Bye", "Step pon Chi Chi Man" and "We Nuh Like Gay" tunes blaring from the dancehall since the late 1990s are cultural phenomena that re-present the creeping fear of male feminization through the lens of anti–male homosexual lyrics. Male homosexuality is threatening because it tampers with the definitions of masculine identity through sex and sexual identity where manhood has been traditionally defined as male domination over women. Therefore, the radical anti–male homosexual paranoia that exists in Jamaica and within the dancehall dis/place is signified by the paucity of dancehall songs that violently denounce lesbianism and the corresponding surfeit of songs and lyrics that denounce male homosexuality. Dancehall songs of the chi-chi man genre are rife with narratives in which male homosexuals are stereotyped, labelled, nicknamed, disrespected, burnt, stabbed, beaten, run out of town, shot and killed in a variety of creative and excruciating fashions. These male fantasies provide a cathartic release for the tensions and fears that exist about male homosexuality and its negative effects on the negotiation of masculine identity; they also sound a warning bell to "all dem gays deh" that male homosexuality will not be tolerated in Jamaica as there are many willing and able defenders of true manhood.

As opportunities increase for educational advancement, more women are availing themselves of post-secondary, professional and tertiary education. The resultant over-supply of highly educated women in Jamaica has become a cause for concern as to the future effects on the status and identity of men. Statistics from the Mona campus of the University of the West Indies over the last ten years have revealed a growing increase in the percentage of female graduates (over 70 per cent) against a declining percentage for men. As the social and economic fall-out in Jamaica gathers momentum, the groups of beggars and hustlers at stop-lights, parking lots, shopping malls and street corners in Kingston and St Andrew are increasingly male. Clashes with the police inevitably have male fatalities and the prisons are full of men. Many Jamaican men have been and continue to be socialized into a patently patriarchal framework[56] that claims to issue resources to them based solely on their masculinity. In today's Jamaica, the reality is that resources are allocated based on one's identity-negotiation around the rigid race/class/colour social hierarchy existing in Jamaica. This negotiation also has to contend with external, global factors and the impact of free-market capitalism. In this free-market capitalist framework, the eternal dollar is king and the labour force is asexual.

The real and perceived psychological barriers which exist for many Jamaican men based on the economic constraints and the corruption of historically dated gender identities results in more women succeeding in improving their lives by utilizing their increased access to resources at all levels. On the other hand, the constrained definitions of black masculinity that exist in Jamaica result in the perception that the black, working-class man has fewer choices because many escape routes are invalidated or delegitimized by his definitions of masculinity.

Within the dancehall dis/place, these manifestations and sites of contestation are invariably focused around the feminine. For example, these tensions are encoded in the conquering and courtship of the feared punaany and the pitting of wife against matie, to the elevating of woman/wife over skettel. They are also manifested and contested in the consistent battle against male homosexuality – the violent denunciation of the male homosexual labelled battyman, gay or chi-chi man.

The primary role that both sex and sexuality play in underpinning gendered identities at different levels in Jamaican society becomes more important when material resources are increasingly denied or inaccessible to particular groups of men on the one hand, and become increasingly accessible to women on the other. In this framework, the operation of traditional hierarchies of race/class/colour further the creation and re-presentation of gendered notions of self and personhood in the dancehall dis/place. Dancehall narratives of gendered identity that identify the high profile, aggressive independent ooman whose economic mobility and independence allows her to choose her male partner and dominate in intimate, sexual relationships are balanced by those that proliferate about the dependent matie and sexually promiscuous skettel who remain the pawn of dominant and clever male courtiers and conquerors. In a similar vein, these male courtiers and conquerors wax lyrical about the offensive chi-chi man, battyman or gay guy whose existence becomes more significant because of the creeping erasure of traditional elements that once underlay the foundation of gendered identities. Several factors, which include new developments in the media, the informal sector and the educational arena, together with a mixture of social practices including "female headship, independence, and assertiveness are in flagrant contradiction with culturally held beliefs and contribute to a sense of male insecurity with respect to manhood".[57] It is arguable that these and other factors also impact the overwhelming volume of violent narratives that are a part of dancehall discourse.

Bigging Up Dons and Shottas: Violence in the Dancehall

IN THE DANCEHALL, violence is manifested in the lyrics of the songs and portrayed in the interaction between dancehall artistes onstage, between artiste and audience, and among audience members. Deejays such as Ninjaman, the Original Gold Teeth, Front Teeth, Gun Pon Teeth Don Gorgon; Supercat, the Wild Apache/Don Dadda; Josey Wales, the Bad Bwoy Colonel; and Bounty Killer, the Warlord/Poor People Defender (now renamed the Ghetto Gladiator) are members of a select cadre linked to the promulgation and romanticizing of violence. The glamorized image of violence that these men re-present in dancehall music culture is heralded by their monikers, many of which speak to the "Hollywoodization" of Jamaican popular culture. The gun is an offensive or defensive weapon but is as well a symbol of liberation and masculine or personal power. It is also a tool of extreme and final violence that has remained one critical component of the performances in this male-dominated music culture and continues to be reified and uplifted in the lyrics and performance of many contemporary deejays.[1] Their allegedly close involvement with guns and violence in their real social relations, coupled with their role as dancehall artistes and cultural griots, means that while staging and mimicking violence in the dancehall these artistes are simultaneously involved in making meanings of social and political practices that form a part of Jamaican inner-city reality and dancehall world view.

Within the wider Jamaican society, force and violence have long been a vibrant part of the country's political history and culture. There are noted instances of the liberating use of violence in the numerous slave revolts against the British colonists, including the 1833 Christmas rebellion led by Sam Sharpe and the 1865 Morant Bay Rebellion led by Paul Bogle, as well as the 1938 upheavals when Jamaican workers rioted against low wages and severe working and living conditions.[2] In the post-independence era, violence in the Jamaican society escalated significantly and can be disaggregated into six distinct types: violent crimes, political violence, drug violence, domestic violence, inter-personal violence and gang violence.[3]

Fuelled by the fallout of structural adjustment, criminal activity in Jamaica underwent restructuring in the late 1980s: the accelerated trade in marijuana as traffickers sought to exploit the economic political crisis facing the country and the resort to organized high-intensity political violence as the country became ideologically polarized under the PNP and JLP political parties. This restructuring of criminal activity has, over time, resulted in declining levels of property crimes and increasing levels of violent and fatal crimes. Violent crimes increased by 33 per cent from 1974 to 1996 while property crimes decreased by 55 per cent. Other crimes such as fraud, drug crimes and illegal possession of guns all increased by 1 per cent, 3 per cent and 14 per cent respectively for the same period.[4] This consistent increase in violent and fatal crimes is the main factor that underpins the disorienting fear and near panic that characterizes the debate around crime in Jamaica.

Violence as a phenomenon is not confined to Jamaica's urban centres or among its poor people. Nonetheless, more attention is paid to violent crime and this type tends to be geographically concentrated in poor, urban communities. More than half of all violent crimes committed in Jamaica are concentrated in the urban centres of Kingston and St Andrew, with other urbanized areas in St Catherine and St James accounting for large figures. During the period 1984 to 1992, total crime aggregates were 20,715 in Kingston, 40,756 in St Andrew, 22,105 for St Catherine and 10,816 for St James. Whereas St Andrew records the highest number of serious crimes, disaggregated figures show that Kingston Central's crime rate of 7,075 was the highest per capita for the entire period. In the 1950s and 1960s, murder rates for Jamaica were approximately 7 per 100,000 persons. By 1980, this had increased to 236.[5] Between 1961 and 1963, the number of murders was 183 and this figure ballooned to a reported 981 cases in 1989–90.[6]

The 1997 World Bank report on Jamaica noted that violence exacerbated poverty and that urban poverty could lead to increased violence. In relation to the inner cities of Kingston, the report noted that lack of employment creates violence differentiated by gender. For men, especially young men, unemployment, frustration and idleness often result in gang involvement, violence and encounters with the police. For women, a lack of income increases their dependence on men and often results in early and multiple pregnancies. This in turn results in domestic violence aimed at partners and children. The study linked poor, inadequate or a total lack of parenting skills, especially among young parents, to observable violent tendencies in their children, who later tended to become violent adults. Inadequate and poor housing conditions accompanied by the overcrowding associated with poor, urban communities further concentrated several social problems into these confined areas, resulting in an aggravation of and an increase in violence.

The 1980s emergence and rise to popularity of dancehall artistes from the bowels of Kingston's inner cities provided a stage on which individuals could lyrically and symbolically project an intense fascination with different forms of violence – gun violence, sexual violence, violence against women, as well as violence against self and society. The images of violence that are disseminated by these artistes have been identified as purely metaphorical: a kind of lyrical, social commentary.[7] My own research in the belly of the dancehall reveals that this lyrical violence is often tenuously linked to real acts of violence, particularly when dancehall narratives reflect the realities of violence in Kingston's inner cities. The close relationship between lyrical and real violence is particularly evident within the sociopolitical and economic realities of the inner cities, because the lives and practices of individuals in these communities impact directly on the flood of violent symbols and messages that are emitted in the dancehall's lyrical and cultural output.

As the dancehall dis/place developed from the early days of the 1980s into the 1990s, the violence that was idealized and symbolized in its lyrical outpourings and interaction of the stage-audience and audience-stage dialogue moved farther away from the type of violence encoded in the reggae music that infused the earlier genre of Jamaican popular culture in the 1970s. This was the *rude bwoy* era typified by the character Rhyghin in the movie *The Harder They Come*. Ivanhoe Martin, the model for the role that Jimmy Cliff played in the movie, had become famous around 1948 as the ultimate *rudie*, following a series of gun battles with the police.[8] In the movie, Rhyghin was a rural transplant to the urban centre of Kingston whose ultimate ascent (or descent) into rude bwoy status parodied the hopes and dreams of many poor, young men from the rural areas of Jamaica who left their homes to seek their fortunes in the city during the promising post-independence era. Many of these rural-urban migrants ended up with their dreams shattered, ultimately unemployed in the shanty towns of Kingston. The increasing numbers of unemployed, frustrated young men was one important reason for the growth of lawlessness in Kingston. Rhyghin's transformation into a gunman is romanticized and he becomes the typical, male folk hero who simultaneously claims his identity while transgressing the accepted social order. The popular culture narratives of the 1960s and 1970s captured and reified the popularized image of the fearless and violent rude bwoy.[9] Rude bwoy music was aimed specifically at the ghetto youth and included songs like Joe White's "Rudies All Around", the Wailers's early single "Simmer Down", Keith McCarthy's "Everybody Rude Now", and the Clarendonians's "Rudie Gone a Jail" and "Rudie Bam Bam".[10]

In its own historical and conjunctural moment, the dancehall responded to and negotiated the slippery slopes of change in post–structural adjustment Jamaica. The offensive weapon of choice discussed in the dancehall moved away from the cold steel of the knife and oriented itself around a more powerful, destructive and deadly weapon – the gun. From the 1980s onwards, the warm lead of the gun as a weapon of extreme and fatal violence became increasingly more accessible to inner-city youths in Jamaica. Correspondingly, the role of the gun became more important in the male-dominated space of dancehall culture.

Like the gangsta artistes of the related hip-hop genre, *badman* dance-hall griots such as Ninjaman, Supercat, Joey Wales and Bounty Killer claim to draw on their own experiences in their extensive treatises about the virtues of the gun as power. In so doing, they extend the dancehall dis/place's dalliance with violent, gun-filled images and uplift the image and reality of the gun as a route to personal power. Commenting on this tendency in his 1999 lecture on the problems in the cultivation of Jamaican male identity, Chevannes identified the gun as a symbol of young male identity and notes that the "proliferation of guns is not simply a function of the drug trade but the ultimate representation of what it means to be a man".[11] In dancehall music, particular songs become identified as the ultimate badman tunes not only because of their threatening lyrics, but also because their staccato or boom-boom rhythms mimic the sound of individually discharged gunshots or the steady patter from a submachine gun.

For example, Bounty Killer's "Lodge" is a threatening and deadly gun tune, which remains a symbolic anthem for all (gun)men and aspirants in the space of the dancehall. Shabba Ranks's "Shine an Kris" is another in this genre. When these songs are played at a dancehall event, the momentary focus is on the real, hardcore badmen and gunmen in attendance who unhesitatingly signify their agreement with Bounty Killer that "fi mi gun nuh join lodge and it nuh join church". Therefore, if there is any "disrespect, smaddy gwine lie ah dirt". Bounty Killer dishes out these words in harsh, aggressive and staccato vocals (reminiscent of machine gunfire) over the Stalag 17 rhythm made famous in Tenor Saw's 1985 "Ring the Alarm". These same badmen also affirm Shabba Ranks's cool and deadly exhortation to "oil up all ah di gun dem, keep dem shine an kris". Videographers and photographers are aware of the fact that that these are badman tunes which signify the ideal time to feature "some gunman and some badman"[12] when they indicate their assent and identification with the powerful and deadly themes of these songs by hands raised in a pointing gun salute, waves, flags, flaring lighters and the occasional discharge of live rounds of ammunition.

Here, the phenomenon of the rude bwoy is useful in crafting a comparative examination of how the use of violent, criminal messages and imagery in popular cultural narratives aims to open spaces of liberty in a socially, politically and economically repressed context. In the first instance, the rude bwoy narratives were aimed primarily at the dispossessed and frustrated rural men and boys whose dreams of wealth and mobility lay shattered in the shanty towns of Kingston. In the second instance, the violent narratives of the dancehall that glamorize the dons and shottas provide a positive-negative pole around which young men from Kingston's inner cities can orient and claim their dreams of status and mobility behind the barrel of a gun. Yet, the similarities and differences between Rhyghin, the 1970s rude bwoy and folk hero of *The Harder They Come,* and Priest, the criminally deviant shotta in the Island Records movie *Dancehall Queen,* highlight the political perceptions of the dynamics of change operating within Jamaican popular culture and ghetto culture, as well as within the wider Jamaican society. The rude bwoy of the 1970s was portrayed as a romantic, heroic folk figure, exemplified in the movie *The Harder the Come* and parodied by various artistes of that era in their musical offerings about rudies. The persona of a rudie was anti-systemic and encapsulated varying levels of ideological and social power: power that had a limited effect on the tight social and political control of the status quo in the wider society of that era. Like the rudies, today's anti-heroes of violence in the dancehall dis/place have deep-rooted linkages with inner cities and poverty. However, as a part of the conjunctural symbols of dancehall's specific historical moment, its deviant heroes are also intertwined with symbols of political tribalism, narco-culture and gun culture. Consequently, the ideological and social power of dancehall's violent icons has deepened beyond popular culture's narrative idealization of the real badman. This is particularly related to the growing economic, political and cultural power of the high status dons, area leaders and shottas from the inner cities of Kingston who use the threat and practice of gun violence and intimidation as tools in the maintenance of their hold over various inner-city communities.

"Don" is a title of distinction afforded to men who are considered to be of high social, political and economic status in Jamaica. It is particularly used to denote status among men from the lower socioeconomic levels and in the inner-city context. The term is commonly used in inner-city and dancehall slang and its definition draws significantly from the distinctive label given to Mafia overlords of the kind immortalized in the film *The Godfather*. The Jamaican term, however, is oriented around indigenous symbols of the ghetto gunman who may sometimes have political or narco-political linkages. Political dons are affiliated to one of the two major political parties in Jamaica (the ruling PNP or the opposition JLP) and generally oversee the running of garrison communities in Jamaica. Many prominent dons have been accused of illegal or extra-legal activities such as extortion and drug-running. Christopher Charles and Charles Price note that the don typically provides social welfare and informal justice services in their communities.[13]

The area leader is hierarchically related to but different from the don. The area leader becomes prominent and influential in the community because of his or her hard work and the respect engendered as a facilitator of community development.[14] The area leader may subsequently acquire enough social, political and economic resources to accede to the higher position of don. It is important to note that while some women become area leaders, there are no female dons in Jamaica. Therefore, there is a hierarchical and gendered relationship between dons and area leaders. All dons are area leaders but not all area leaders become dons, and all dons are male while there are a few female area leaders.

It is also important to note that the political allegiance of many dons to one of Jamaica's two main political parties (PNP or JLP) evolved out of the political relationships of the 1970s. The deepening partisan, political violence of the 1970s was underwritten by the thriving patron-clientelist system based on the distribution of political largesse and resources from the members of the formal political structure (members of parliament, councillors) to their henchmen in these and other communities.[15] This created a yawning space for the rise of the dons and area leaders, who developed first as lackeys of this feudal-type political structure and who ruled inner-city and garrison communities on behalf of their overlords, the political leaders who held constituency representational rights in the formal political structure. The role of these dons was to ensure the continued dominance of a particular individual at the polls by any means, as well as to keep the community unified against intruders, political and otherwise – again, by any means. Dons also organized and distributed to members of their communities the largesse passed on to them by their political bosses. The role of guns as central to the authority of the dons assumed primacy in this era as dons reportedly received guns from their political bosses to assist in the carrying out of their duties.

The fall-out from the imposition of structural adjustment policies and the resultant contraction and transformations in Jamaica's socioeconomic arena in the 1980s[16] also resulted in a change in the role, practice and authority of the dons. Some important dons had been betrayed by their bosses and either killed or sent to prison, thus opening the way for the rise of their area leaders to positions of prominence and power. Like the dons, the area leaders maintained the unity and cohesion of the community and preserved it as a massive homogeneous voting bloc on behalf of one political party during elections. Some area leaders were promoted to donship. However, the fall-out of structural adjustment resulted in a significant reduction in the available political largesse that could be doled out to faithful and loyal supporters of these political parties. This created a series of shifts in the former patron-clientelist system. The lack of economic support and withering away of largesse from the formal political arena created a wide economic gap. The former economic dependence of the dons and area leaders on their political overlords was transferred to the informal structures that rose up in response to the harsh economic climate that developed after the fall-out of structural adjustment. With the rise of the higglers and ICIs, increased migration and the growth of the illegal narco-culture, the dons and area leaders were able to access local and international resources above and beyond that being offered by the political patron or boss.[17] This consequently resulted in a decline in the authority of the political bosses. Further, the role of immigrants in the diaspora in providing resources (money, guns, clothes, jewellery and so on) to actors in these areas also assisted in the erosion of the authority and role of the political patrons and their henchmen. Harriott notes the high levels of moral authority that local narco-political dons gained from superimposing their own criminal organization on existing political structures.[18]

The 1999 Island movie *Third World Cop* and the 2002 underground DVD release *Shottas* provide glimpses into the existential realities of Kingston's inner cities and highlight the key linkages of dancehall culture to other local and international factors in this framework. The proliferation of guns and the increasingly easy access to them by youths and others successfully eroded the superordinate position of the area leader or don and opened the way for a freelance type of gunman or gang grouping. Rising economic pressures, increased access to illegal guns, an increasing trade in illegal drugs, drug use and abuse, and a steadily increasing crime rate provided the birthing ground for the phenomenon of the shotta. *Shotta* is the Jamaican Creole word for "shooter". The term rose to prominence in the dancehall culture in late 1998. Charles defines the shottas as the gunmen in the informal party militias and the organized criminal gangs that are controlled by the don.[19] Additionally, I define shottas as independent inner-city gunmen who operate without the structural constraints of a defined gang. While gunwomen may exist, they are not popularized in inner-city and dancehall myths. The shottas are gun-toting men who are ranked lowest on the continuum of the violent masculinities that exist in inner-city and garrison culture. In Jamaican dancehall and inner-city culture, the addition of the prefix "top" or "don" adds more seniority and respect to the title. Like the image of the don, the image of the individualistic and materialistic shotta is highly romanticized in dancehall music and culture. The shotta, a direct descendant of the rude bwoy of the 1970s and a legitimate offspring of the don, represents a conjunction of different and related factors including reduction of political largesse in a declining economy; access to guns and money from various sources; a thriving local-international trade in illegal drugs; and the instant-gratification ethos that has overtaken a growing sector of Jamaican youth.

There has also been a lessening of cohesion and unity within many of these inner-city communities as individual actors work in the underground economy for and on their own behalf. This has proven detrimental to the community network and, in many inner cities, inter-community warfare has developed to such extreme levels that people living at the top of one street are constantly at war with people at the bottom. Many of these poverty-stricken communities operate without the full co-operation or protection of the state and its agents: the police. Therefore, many residents rely on area leaders and dons for security and protection. This lack of unity means that any outsider can enter the community and be disrespectful to or take advantage of its residents. The men with more status, like the area leader, cannot control the young men, because most of these young men have their own guns and are unwilling to defer to the authority of these "older heads". During my own research in one Kingston inner-city community, several young men in their early to mid-teens explained that they wanted to "run" their street or lane and "protect" their friends and family members from intruders or outsiders. They described instances when "war bruk out" and men, women and children from this small community were shot to death for some insignificant reason. For example, a shotta from one street in the community had "cut up" another youth from their own avenue. They said that the intense war and battle that raged over this incident took the lives of four young men, one woman and two children before it was quelled. In another instance, a group of younger shottas who had "gotten their own guns" decided to rob a group of cocaine vendors who operated along Spanish Town Road, an area outside the environs of their own community. After committing the robbery and returning to their community, they were pounced upon by another group of shottas from their own community and robbed. The more mature gang leaders and "older heads" in the community tried to mediate and quell the impending war, but the two groups of young shottas "bruk out" into a raging battle that took the lives of more than ten persons over a two-week period. Paradoxically, while some people in these and other communities state that they are paralysed by fear because of the high rate of gun crimes, affectors and affectees in the dancehall dis/place play a significant role in glamorizing, reinforcing and promoting the persona and identity of the don, area leader or shotta.

Within this context, the contemporary personification of violence in the dancehall dis/place – the shotta – is self-formed and self-cultivated, an entrepreneur in a free-market, capitalist framework. With the existing corruption in the variables that denote a masculine identity or full manhood, the shotta becomes one route to this ascendancy. As the full realization of masculine identity becomes less and less associated with honest work or gainful employment and more with money and symbols of wealth, the self-employed, entrepreneurial shotta enjoys high levels of moral authority and respect in inner-city communities. Further, the shotta is deified and perceived as a heroic figure by young inner-city men, some of whom aspire to this superordinate position. Easy access to ille-gal guns has only served to reinforce the practice of gun-play as a route to masculinity.

Within dancehall culture, the term "shotta", like that of the violent clashmaster, has masculine and positive connotations. It is masculine because it is rooted in the personification of a man carrying a gun, a gunman, a male in the same genre as the don or rude bwoy of earlier vin-tage. It is positive because of the perception of this individual as a man who upholds the patriarchal ideals of masculine power, aggressiveness and strength. This patriarchal ideal is further enhanced by the hard, phallic power that resides in the image of a gun – a symbolic and perpet-ually erect penis.

For example, the "shotta youths" are those younger males who engage in questionable gun-related activities or simply those who are deemed worthy of great respect based on their economic or personal standing in their communities. Although it is primarily identified as mas-culine, the term "don" is also used to accord respect to women as with the "donnette" (feminine derivative of "don") or rude girl (feminine derivative of rude bwoy) of earlier vintage. In similar vintage, the "shotta girl" or "shotta woman" is usually a female who is perceived as aggres-sive, independent and ambitious.

The shottas are highly respected in the dancehall dis/place and at many dancehall stage shows and events the sound system operator usu-ally announces the arrival of authority figures to the dancehall in order to ensure that all individuals of high status are acknowledged. The shot-tas, as part of this group, are consistently featured:

> Big up all di shotta dem inna di dance. Man like —— and ——. And big up di shotta crew from dung a —— an di man dem from —— and mi brethren fresh from outa New York di man call —— nuff respect.

> (Accolades and respect go out to all of the shooters present at this dance. For example, —— and ——. Also accolades and respect to the group of shooters from down by —— and all the men from —— and to my friend who just recently arrived from New York by the name of ——, a great deal of respect to you.)

The code of silence is very much a part of the give and take of the dis/place and it often subsumes key linkages between actors in the dance-hall and individuals who are key activists in drug and gun culture. More often than not, the philanthropic activities of these shottas within the inner-city communities of their origin and the broader dis/place have resulted in their appropriation of high levels of social power within these communities. They are viewed as providers, defenders and "police" by many residents.

Beyond the confines of the dancehall dis/place and in the wider Jamaican society, the shotta is viewed both negatively and positively depending on the age, social class and educational level of the individual. Some young people, up to the secondary school level and some at the tertiary level, also perceive shottas in a positive light. To this extent, teenage girls will adopt the label of "shotta girl Annette" or become members of groups known as the "shotta girls". Teenage boys struggling to define their masculinity are also influenced by this definition, since one is granted status and accolade if one is labelled "shotta Mark" or "shotta Kareem". This perception is shared by young people from both rural and urban working- and middle-class backgrounds who view the image of the shotta as part of the recurring hype of dancehall music and culture.

During the initial period of this research, the symbolic acceptance of the term "top shotta" was further replicated on the windscreens of some vehicles plying the Kingston Metropolitan Region between Kingston, St Andrew and St Catherine. One public passenger vehicle, a bus on the Spanish Town to Cross Roads route, goes by the name Top Shotta. Many regular passengers on this vehicle agreed that Top Shotta was the bus to take if one wished to get to and from work within a reasonable time. One passenger noted that Top Shotta takes fifteen minutes between Spanish Town and Half Way Tree regardless of the time of day or level of congestion on the roads. This was attributed to the fact that the bus driver did not obey any rules of the road nor did he respect other drivers. His aggressive and careless driving practices meant that other users of the roads were literally forced to give way to this bus. Yet, Top Shotta remained a real favourite with young people and others who enjoyed its loud, dancehall music and its timely journeys back and forth.

Conversely, other Jamaicans perceive the "shotta" phenomenon in a negative light. They deem this name as symbolic of the glorification of gun violence and gunmen. It represents, for many, creeping ghetto culture taking over decent Jamaica and contributing significantly to the increasing crime rate. The shottas are viewed as criminals, aggressors and political terrorists.

Yet the organic link that ties garrison/inner-city lifestyle and culture to dancehall culture means that the trajectory of rude bwoy to area leader to don to shotta is superimposed on the lyrics and parodied in the performances of the dancehall. As a result, the trajectory of violent identities that are parodied and performed in Jamaican popular culture run the gamut from rude bwoy of the 1970s to the don or area leader of the 1980s, 1990s and beyond to the shotta of contemporary fame. This trajectory of (gun) violence in dancehall narratives represents real social and political battles in Jamaica, particularly within in the inner cities. In the dancehall of the early 1980s, artistes Tiger (Norman Jackson), Ninjaman (Desmond Ballentine) and Supercat (Wayne Maragh) released songs that discussed dons. In his song "Don Is Don, Donovan Donovan", Tiger paid homage to Jamaican masculinity by using a discourse that proclaimed Jamaican men as uncontested leaders and masters in their individual circles. In his own songs, Ninjaman asserted himself as the "Original Gold Teeth, Front Teeth, Gun Pon Teeth Don Gorgon" and Supercat responded by declaring himself a "Don Dadda". The term "don" became a referent among patrons of the Jamaican dancehall and the wider society, helped along by its widespread usage and constant citation in the electronic and print media. Further, the terms "don" and "donmanship" gained widespread popularity, usage and ultimately popular immortality when Edward Seaga, leader of the JLP responded to factions and mutinous disaffection among his party members in the mid-1980s by publicly proclaiming himself as the "One Don" of the party. The fact that for nearly four decades Seaga had successfully maintained his position as elected member of parliament for the Western Kingston garrison constituency that houses Tivoli Gardens had particular resonance for this declaration. Lloyd Lovindeer immortalized Seaga's declaration in his humorous song, "Light a Candle (Find Your Way Back Home)", proclaiming that there is "one don alone".

DJ Tiger in a mid-air leap during a stunning and energetic closing act on Dancehall Night, Reggae Sunsplash 1989. Courtesy of the Gleaner Company Limited.

Dancehall narratives and performance depict the don or shotta as a being whose entire existence is circumscribed and defined by violence, deviance and lawlessness. This narrative depiction is solidified by the lyrical, symbolic and physical (facial contortions, body posture, style of dress and way of speaking) mimicry of violence in which select male artistes and their supporters in the dancehall engage.

Of all the dancehall artistes who declared their early donmanship, Ninjaman remains as one noteworthy example of a veteran, hardcore, dancehall artiste who has consistently relied on use of violent lyrics and imagery in his dancehall performance while simultaneously projecting a persona that is declared lawless and deviant based on his famed brushes with the law. Ninjaman's performances at two dancehall events, Sting 2003 and 2004, are useful examples of his contemporary use of the dancehall stage to project and perform violence.

The intertwined narratives of violence and popular culture accord significant levels of power and approval to the images of the shotta and his predecessors in the dis/place. This cultural approval is in direct contestation with traditional middle-class mores in Jamaica. The projected pat-

DJ Ninja Man holds a New Testament Bible given to him by a patron during his performance on Dancehall Night, Reggae Sunsplash 1993. Courtesy of the Gleaner Company Limited.

terns of power and identity within these lived realities – the *livity* of actors within this cultural dis/place – compete and contrast with the lived reality of traditional Jamaica. At the same time, my own research reflects the ambivalence that many affectors and affectees have for these images of violence, since the images may display behaviours and attitudes that contradict their own responses to and statements about violence in dancehall and the wider society. For many such actors it is a "dancehall thing" and they will signify their assent to the gun tunes and violent performances at the dancehall event but will revert to a state of disgust with high levels of crime and gun violence in the society once they have left the event.

Boundaries of Violence in the Dancehall

The boundaries of violence in the dancehall shift and become more permeable and porous in particular instances. In these places and spaces, the tenuous link between lyrical and real violence often becomes frayed, resulting in confrontations between individuals. For example, a dancehall stage show or session can become the mediated environment for the staging of interpersonal, intra-gang and drug wars. These include matie wars, where women try to upstage each other for primary positions as wife/woman number one. These symbolic parodies of costume and dress within the performative event are one move away from embattled, hand-over-hand duels and street fights. Rival narco-political dons or rival gangs also use the performative space of the dancehall event to wage their battles and upstage their competitors in a very public and highly dramatized moment. This ensures adequate publicity and legitimizing of the primary position of the man or group who emerges as winner at one publicized moment in the dancehall dis/place.

Sometimes, deejays use this space to engage in lyrical battles with their competitors and these lyrical battles onstage result in violent and physical confrontations offstage. Here, the positions of ascendancy of the lyrical dons are defended in an overtly violent fashion as these high positions of status and power in the dancehall afford them real moral authority and power within their communities and in the wider dancehall arena. This is accompanied by correspondingly high levels of publicity and access to wealth and status in the wider social environment, both locally and internationally, and symbolizes in very real ways their overturning of the existing sociopolitical and socioeconomic hierarchies in Jamaica.

Deejays like Ninjaman, Bounty Killer, Supercat and Josey Wales, who all become renowned as "Masters of the Lyrical Clash", embody the aspirations and hopes of their marginalized siblings in the dis/place who remain stuck in their violated spaces. Therefore, as members of the violated masses who subsequently ascend into the public spaces of the violators, the role and identity of clashmasters, who inevitably become known as violent deejays in the wider social environment, is critical in ensuring the cathartic release of the confined aspirations and emotions of their marginalized siblings. These clashmasters have moved up and moved out of their confined dis/places without utilizing the dead-end routes prescribed by traditional Jamaican society. Therefore, the interaction between clashmasters and their "victims", who are lyrically "killed" or "murdered" onstage during a dancehall performance event, either during an ongoing lyrical tango or in absentia, is paralleled by the interactive support (shouts, gun salutes, flaring cigarette lighters, fire torches, screams, waved flags and so on) and ideological support of the live audience. Affectees who are absent from this lyrical battle can use the electronic media to participate in this interaction (videocassette, audiocassette, cable television or newspaper report). These absent affectees also engage in interactive (screams, accolades, facial and bodily contortions) and ideological support of these actions when they participate.

The blurred boundaries of violent interaction between the lyrical clashmaster and his victim (onstage or in absentia); between the clashmaster and the live audience; among individual members of the live audience; and between individual members of the live audience and guardians of the sociopolitical boundaries of decent and non-violent behaviour, for example, police and security guards, become more permeable and porous in specific and definitive spaces. The following discussions of the midsummer Reggae Sunsplash (which gave way to Reggae Sumfest), the end of year Sting and the overview of Border Clash 1990 are useful examples of the variations of violent interaction at a dancehall event.

Reggae Sunsplash (Sumfest)

From the outset, the hosting of Reggae Sunsplash in the tourist mecca of Montego Bay, St James, created an association with a local middle/upper-class and foreign tourist audience. The thrust for support inevitably focused on these groupings and defined the range and formats of performer-audience interaction that existed at this event. With the coining of the term "Dancehall Night" and its first staging in 1982, the Synergy-led Reggae Sunsplash created a space for the increasingly popular local grassroots and inner-city audience who enjoyed the music and/or subscribed to the world view of the dancehall dis/place. This space existed within boundaries that were denoted and circumscribed by the markers of "decent" and traditional Jamaican mores. I acknowledge the broader space allocated to the deejays in disseminating their lyrical outpourings and in their abilities to clash lyrically or physically with other dancehall artistes at this type of event. Yet the space allocated for the reaffirmation of the dancehall adherents was carefully bounded and reduced the boundaries of interplay that could exist between audience and stage and among audience members. It therefore reduced the violent interplay that often accompanied performative events in the dancehall dis/place. Several factors contributed to this containment.

One contributing factor was the overwhelming presence of particular groups of people identified as higher on the sociopolitical ladder. These included white overseas tourists, upper- and middle-class Jamaicans, and the overarching presence of members of the Jamaica Constabulary Force and private security personnel. Many of these individuals were easily identified by their skin colour, mode of dress, manner of speaking and general demeanour. These individuals provided a high concentration of identities whose roles acted as markers of traditional constraint.

Another factor that helped to delimit the boundaries of violence at Reggae Sunsplash was that the hosting of the event during the height of the summer months in August reflected an overt identification with the mores of tourists, be they upper-/middle-class Jamaican or foreigners. These are individuals whose social positions meant that they could afford the economic privilege of taking a vacation. Many of these people transformed the entire week of reggae activities into a vacation in Montego Bay. On the contrary, the lower-class, grassroots and inner-city Jamaican adherent of dancehall culture could usually afford to pay for only one night of participation in this reggae festival. The majority opted for a celebration of their burgeoning transformation within the dis/place. Dancehall Night, hosted on the Thursday night of each Reggae Sunsplash, inevitably drew the largest crowds as the regular support of the monied classes was backed by the momentary support of adherents of the dancehall. In 1987, almost 40,000 individuals crammed into the Bob Marley Performing Centre on Dancehall Night, with approximate figures of 35,000 in 1988 and 25,000 in 1989 for the same night. For

Reggae Sunsplash 1989, Monday's Final Sound System Clash Night saw a meagre 3,000 individuals attending; Tuesday's Beach Party Night a little under 5,000; Wednesday night, billed as a tribute to two greats, saw a little under 10,000; Friday's Singers' night, 15,000; and International Night gained just under 20,000 people in attendance.[20]

Another factor that contributes to lower levels of violence at Reggae Sunsplash is its geographical location. The hosting of this event in the city of Montego Bay on the north-west coast meant that it was far removed from the realities of the inner cities of Kingston and St Andrew in the south-east, even though this was and remains the spawning ground for dancehall music and the primary home of members of the dis/place. This meant that those members of the audience who identified with the clashmasters onstage had to filter this identification process through the lens of physical space and distance. Many residents of inner-city communities travel overseas more frequently and with more ease than they do in the urban-rural passages out of Kingston or St Andrew. This is so because, in Jamaica, many lack the self-confidence and self-esteem to travel too far beyond the local communities that provide a comforting frame of reference for their own notions of personhood.

The foregoing factors served to create a particular event profile that actively delimits and polices the level of violence that can erupt. This meant that most of the violence is lyrical and symbolic and that few confrontations take place. For example, in 1989, when deejay Ninjaman ruled the dancehall as master of the clash, Dancehall Night erupted into lyrical and real violence but this was carefully policed and controlled.

I attended this 1989 Dancehall Night and, like many dancehall stage shows then and now, the early performances of less renowned artistes set the stage for the dancehall greats, whose arrival would be heralded by a final band change to Sagittarius (King Saggi), the then supreme dancehall band with the Vibesmaster, Derek Barnett,[21] on bass guitar. The night progressed from this first tier (backed by the band Kotch) into the second tier – heralded by the corresponding band change to the Riddim Kings – and the artiste flow included more popular artistes like Shelly Thunder, Admiral Tibet, Sanchez and Flourgon.

The audience make-up also shifted during this progression of artistes onstage. The front-stage audience that had earlier enjoyed wider limits of individual space and some passable levels of camaraderie became increasingly more clustered, tense and less jocular. A newer and less approachable persona interspersed itself into the openings, combining body force and an overtly menacing aura to enclose the front-stage audience in a cocoon of tension and aggression. "Excuse me, you are stepping on my towel," timidly remarked one white tourist to an overweight woman clad in tight, skimpy, spandex shorts and a brassiere-like top, combined with a corona of purple hair ascending skywards. "Ooman!" replied the overweight woman, "Mi pay fi come in yaso an yuh nuh own no way yaso. Move yuh sitten dem if yuh nuh waan nubady walk pan dem" (Woman! I paid to come in here and you do not own anyplace here. Move your things if you do not want anyone to walk on them). This reply was accompanied by a defensive grunt, a daring shrug of the shoulders and an aggressive facial contortion. Grunts of assent from a group of similarly clad women ready to rally to the defence of their companion forced the tourist to retrieve her towel and retreat hastily. These women were accompanied by groups of men (young and middle-aged) whose style of clothing, forceful body language and overemphasized use of street-slang were clearly alligned with an urban, inner-city aesthetic.

Backstage the flow of bodies was also transformed. A burgeoning number of dancehall artistes now complemented the earlier congestion of media personnel, Sunsplash personnel, sponsors, tourists, artistes and middle- and upper-class individuals. These artistes each headed an entourage of men and women, whose flashy, outrageous and colourful style of dress identified them as individuals whose lifestyles were circumscribed by dancehall culture. The carefully staged entrance, flashy dressing and stylized body movements of these individuals were matched only by their vocal enunciations as they engaged in the ritualistic posing and posturing that characterizes the dancehall. This spectacular exhibition ensured that they were treated with the respect afforded to individuals whose status within dancehall culture allowed them acquisition of a coveted backstage pass. Several minor confrontations developed with the security guards at the backstage entrance because many of these individuals, who felt that they were important enough to be recognized, refused to show their passes and accused the guards of "dissing them".

The announcement of the final band change to the ruling band, King Saggi, heralded the presentation of the dancehall greats and the performative moment which many of the local, Kingston-based and urban inner-city massive had travelled to see. This signalled the moment of self-affirmation with the most prominent of the reigning dancehall artistes. The demanding, forceful physicality and presence of these members of the dancehall body clearly stated that they would not be denied this interaction. Men and women jostled for primacy of space and bodies became weapons of offence and defence. Some used their bodies like battering rams, poking and pushing and seeking to appropriate preferred spaces from which they could view, interact with and revel in the spectacle that was being exhibited onstage. Other bodies merged to become hard, impenetrable barriers, defending and protecting the positions they had chosen within the pressing crowd of bodies.

The air tensed and pulsed with emotion, like a descending cloud of locusts, and was reflected in the increasing petulance of the dancehall massive. Since each body was afforded just enough space to plant two feet, this was a bad time to be lying on "reggae beds" or towels in proximity to the front. Undoubtedly, this was not the time to step on someone's foot or complain about being jostled or shoved because the slightest provocation could trigger a confrontation. Many unsuspecting individuals fell prey to pickpockets or petty thieves at this time, because the criminals' actions were shielded by the crush of bodies.

Previous forays into the space of Dancehall Night had revealed that it was useful to identify closely with the dominant persona if one wanted to get a good view of the stage. Therefore, all of us in my "country" group informed everyone around us that we came from somewhere in the parish of Kingston. Although our clothing did not match the elaborate, expensive regalia and costume of the true dancehall adherent, our announced social background and language transformation meant that we closely approximated the dominant persona. We were enveloped within the body of the dancehall and this temporary transformation served to reduce or eliminate conflicts that could develop from simple misunderstandings.

As Dancehall Night 1989 progressed, the final, greatest surge forward of bodies preceded the arrival of the reigning superstar, Ninjaman. Veterans of Dancehall Night used the hiatus between the last performer onstage and Ninjaman's impending arrival onstage to hastily gather together and secure all possessions. All bags and backpacks were strapped firmly into place and reggae beds, towels and other paraphernalia were retrieved from the ground. The continued surge forward was accompanied by entreaties and cajoling statements that entailed veiled threats: "My deejay ah come now, small up yuhself, small up!" (My favourite deejay is coming now, give me room), and "Excuse me, mi ah go up deso. My yout' yuh nuh see mi ah pass?" (Excuse me, I am going right over there. My youth, can't you see that I am trying to pass by you?).

Their stances were threatening and dared anyone to comment on their aggressive body language and forceful and demanding behaviour. Many others who were unwillingly forced to inhabit this explosive moment perceived the composite persona of these aggressive fans as violent, negative, decadent, brutish and bad. Inevitably, many of the white tourists, and some brown and black "decent" members of Jamaican society who had captured these spaces, decided to "small up themselves" or to move away entirely. Some used the privilege afforded by their expensive armbands to go backstage, while others decided to view the proceedings from the fringes and the extreme back section of Bob Marley Performing Centre.

As stealthy and dangerous as a black panther, Ninjaman's surreptitious arrival onstage was hailed with absolute silence and an almost complete paralysis of the audience. Dressed in a black ninja suit, he adopted his signature pose, head cocked at an angle, holding the mike in his right hand and presenting his left hand, palm outward to "his people dem": "One worl ah gun, mi say mi have one worl ah gun" (One/A world of guns, I say that I have one/a world of guns). Roars of adulation and screams of joy were accompanied by a unified thrust and forceful surge forward of the bodies at the extreme front of the audience. Within the confined space, lighters were lit and held aloft, firecrackers were ignited and cast skywards, rags and towels were waved ecstatically and bodies were engaged in a primitive dance of exultation and self-affirmation. The fact that they were also giving assent to gun violence and mayhem seemingly escaped these individuals as they chanted in sync with the deejay: "Shot nuh talk, a kill we kill, / Gundelero write yuh will" (Gunshots do not talk, we kill. / Gunman, write your will). Ninjaman's staccato, violent gun-talk was greeted by roars of agreement from the entire crowd as they crowd united in his frenzied mimicking of violence, exhorting Ninjaman to greater heights of lyrical aggression: "Murda dem, murda dem. / We come yah tonite fi go murda dem" (Murder them, murder them. / We came here tonight to murder them).

That night, as with many others, Ninjaman's role in Jamaican popular culture as an incarnation of violent masculinity that feeds into the social and cultural norms of the society was embodied in his violent, gun-laced lyrical outpourings, his aggressive, warlike demeanor and physical stance as well as his violent interaction backstage with another artiste. In this instance, his confrontation with the Colonel, Josey Wales, was presaged by Wales's lyrical "firing" at Ninjaman during an earlier performance. This lyrical challenge was accepted and contested by Ninjaman in his twice-encored performance during which he made lyrical cuts, thrusts and parries at Wales. This resulted in a physical confrontation backstage between the two; near the end of Ninjaman's performance, he drew a cook's knife but was separated from Wales by backstage hands and police personnel. Ninjaman's final encore onstage was laced with acrid comments and peppered by lyrical volleys fired at Wales as he reminded his adoring fans that he was as bad as or badder than any man in the vicinity. Further confrontations backstage were again halted by the presence of security personnel.

Daybreak descended on the Bob Marley Performing Centre as the dancehall audience exhausted its resources in parodies of violence and exultation and Dancehall Night came to a close. The costumed and bejewelled dancehall massive drifted towards the gates in an effort to secure transportation back to Kingston, St Andrew and elsewhere. The majority had no cars and would have to use public transportation or thumb a ride as they could not pay the exorbitant hotel fees that would afford them some rest before the long journey back home. Yet they had travelled this far to indulge in one night of self-affirmation and self-identification with their icons in the dancehall and had succeeded in grasping one more brilliant moment of personhood within the delimited space of Reggae Sunsplash.

Reggae Sunsplash was finally dissolved in 1994, giving way to Reggae Sumfest which is still held today in Montego Bay, St James. Sumfest is hosted by a group of lighter-skinned, middle-class businessmen who are mainly from Montego Bay. Dancehall Night at Reggae Sumfest continues to operate with the same event profile as its predecessor. To date, this profile continues to delimit and confine the levels of violence that are manifest at this event. However, because of their profile, other major dancehall events, such as Sting, for instance, provide a more porous space for higher levels of violence.

Sting

Sting, a dancehall event hosted by Supreme Promotions, is the major, end-of-year stage show where hardcore dancehall acts are re-presented across the dancehall body. Since its first staging in December 1984, Sting has come to represent the incarnation of crassness, confrontation and violence in dancehall events. It is the event at which the most "almshouse" behaviour is tolerated and encouraged, both onstage and in the audience. Over time, several factors have contributed to this profile.

In the main, the Sting audience is composed of the hardcore adherents of dancehall and inner-city culture, both local and international. Sting's annual staging on Boxing Day means that it is the crowning glory of the dancehall. Performances at Sting are used to introduce new artistes to the dancehall fraternity and to crown the lyrical gladiator for that year. This gladiator's reign in the ensuing year is peppered with lyrical challenges from other aspirants and these drive the dialectical progression of the dancehall for another year. Many dancehall artistes therefore use the months following the summer dancehall events like Reggae Sunsplash or Sumfest to prepare and perfect lyrics that will give them the edge over their rivals at Sting.

Sting, billed as the "Greatest One-Night Reggae Show on Earth", is organized, promoted and hosted by a group of individuals who operate under the name Supreme Promotions. The principals behind Sting include former detective sergeant in the Jamaica Constabulary Force Isaiah Laing; CEO of First Graphic Communications, advertising consultant, lounge singer and director of Supreme Promotions since its inception, Dimario McDowell; entrepreneur Junior "Heavy D" Fraser; and restauranteur and entrepeneur Courtney Bahador. Though these men all have connections to the urban spaces of Kingston and St Andrew and to dancehall culture, Sting is most obviously identified with former police officer and famed crime-fighter, Isaiah Laing. Because of his legendary crime-fighting campaigns against some of Jamaican's most hardened criminals during his years as a police officer in the 1980s and early 1990s, Isaiah Laing has been immortalized in dancehall legend as a "real bad man police" as dancehall artiste Tiger noted in his hit song "When": "Whe di bad man police name? / Laing! / Seen. Come again!" (What is the name of the feared/bad policeman? / Laing! / Yes. Do it again/ Repeat!).

Snowballing from this identification of the premier promoter as a "bad man police", Sting is identified not only as the crowning glory of the dancehall entertainment, but also as the place and space where the audience can expect to consume a special diet of cultural violence with the inevitable lyrical clash between two competing dancehall artistes as its focal point.

In its early days, Sting was held at Cinema 2, an old drive-in theatre in Kingston, and then it moved to the National Stadium. This ensured that Sting remained within easy access to members of the dis/place, many of whom, when it was hosted at the stadium, could take a single bus from their homes and arrive there in less than half an hour. Many could walk to the venue. Because of concerns over its audience size, increasing levels of violence and the threat of damage to the facilities at the National Stadium, Sting was moved to the Jamworld Entertainment Centre in Portmore, St Catherine, in 1993 and has remained at this venue to date. The community of Portmore is contiguous with the larger Kingston Metropolitan Area, thus Sting's easy access to its most significant adherents has been maintained.

The hosting of Sting on Boxing Day (26 December) each year means that it fits neatly into the two-day holiday period in the lives of the inner-city residents. Christmas has special meaning for many Jamaicans, but more so for the marginalized residents of the inner cities. It is the only truly legitimate and fully national public holiday that cuts across all the socioeconomic levels in Jamaican society. It is that one moment when many individuals acquire enough savings or end-of-year bonuses to purchase new clothing as well as expensive food and attend some form of entertainment. For many, it is the time of year when barrels of food and clothing arrive from their friends and relatives in the diaspora. It is also when individuals of high and low status in the diaspora visit and fraternize with their relatives and friends in Jamaica. Indeed, it is a special time of year when those at the higher levels of the local and international illegal drug and gun fraternities return home with huge sums of money and engage in a riotous, bacchanalian, end-of-year celebration of their wealth and status. The Sting audience is this audience. They are not the sun-worshippers, the higher-class or foreign tourist celebrant of that elusive thing called summer. The Sting audience is the underclass and its successful icons whose stints in the informal, underground economy have made them conspicuously wealthy. In its heyday, Sting provided a massive annual backdrop for the conspicuous display of this group's immense wealth. This display held out a promise of future mobility to those who had been left behind in the marginalized dis/places, those who remained stuck in the ghettoes of Kingston.

The physical layout of Sting ensured the audience close physical contact with the performer onstage. Early stagings of Sting at the National Stadium used no chain-link fences or other barriers to separate the audience from front stage and there was no real backstage layout. This meant that in the beginning there was no hierarchical separation of the wider front-stage and backstage audience into varying groups of the privileged over the less privileged as at Reggae Sunsplash or Sumfest. Instead of requiring special passes for entry backstage, this area was not rigidly monitored. Rather, any individual whose regalia, jewellery and self-presentation could identify him or her as a person of high status in the dis/place could gain easy access backstage.

Consequently, Sting's boundaries were almost non-existent, and where they existed, they were much wider. This gave the audience and artistes more freedom to interact with each other. High levels of police presence were associated with the promoters's linkages to the police

A section of the massive crowd at Sting 1991, National Stadium, Kingston. Note the hands held aloft in symbolic gun salutes. Courtesy of the Gleaner Company Limited.

force through Isaiah Laing rather than with a heightened sense of security. In this framework, the levels of violence both on- and offstage at Sting developed and remained higher than at Reggae Sunsplash or Sumfest.

More fights developed at Sting as individuals tried to upstage each other or simply used this space to contest day-to-day personal issues. Gun salutes were loud and frequent and they overshadowed the low tones of the cheaper firecrackers. And at Sting, the use of personal space was limited. This was a one-night event, not part of a week-long festival. Therefore, one could not enjoy the privilege of reggae beds or seats or towels as this event did not facilitate such privileged spatial positioning. Additionally, within the broader spaces of the Sting event, clash-masters indulged in more violent posturings and lyrical outpourings, and the audience acted as an interactive site in the real and lyrical clash.

Border Clash 1990

The clash of borders that has been immortalized in Ninjaman's 1990 dancehall song "Border Clash" was brought forcefully to the attention of individuals within and beyond the dancehall dis/place at the staging of Sting 1991. The popularity of the term "Border Clash" and Ninjaman's successful hit both resulted from a stage show billed as Border Clash that was hosted in 1990 at the then site of Coney Park, the former Ferry Inn (now the site of the Hydel Schools on the Mandela Highway in St Catherine, Jamaica). This Border Clash was billed as a clash between deejays from St Catherine and those from Kingston and St Andrew. The symbolic use of the term "border" and the hosting of this event on the physical border of St Catherine and St Andrew (read Kingston) served to reinforce the physical and ideological barriers that existed between the deejays from either side. The term "clash" encapsulated the expected high levels of lyrical confrontation between the deejays and the divisions between dancehall adherents from different sides of the border. However, the poorly organized event was marred by late and lengthy stage preparation and band set-up. The master of ceremonies, Richie B, was hard-pressed to contain the burgeoning frustration of the audience. This frustration was multilayered because many in the audience felt that they were being cheated, conned and dis-respected by the promoters who were "obviously" unwilling or unable to honour their agreement and present the big name dancehall artistes onstage. The encore performance of famed reggae greats, the Skatalites, added to the frustration.

The dominant form of popular music had shifted radically from roots rock and conscious reggae to dancehall, and the Skatalites were viewed as musical misfits by the dancehall generation. Their twice-repeated performance was the proverbial straw that broke the camel's back and Border Clash erupted as the audience lobbed a veritable rain of glass bottles, forcing the artistes, MC and band members to beat a hasty retreat backstage. Ninjaman saved the day. Secure in his identification as the master of clash and the ultimate Don Gorgon in the dancehall dis/place at that time, he hastily strode onstage holding his left hand aloft and palm outwards in a commanding and placatory gesture. "Hooold on," he cried, instantly transforming the violent mood of the crowd into one of exultation and celebration. His lengthy performance of nearly two hours effectively stemmed the flow of real violence and transformed it into a celebration of lyrical violence. This event and performance presaged the clash of borders at Sting 1991. The Sting profile of lawlessness, unbounded freedom and violence provided the ideological and cultural space for the clash of borders in 1991 which resulted in reggae great Bunny Wailer being physically assaulted by the patrons of the dancehall.

Ruptured Borders at Sting 1991

As noted in the foregoing, the annual hosting of Sting provided a stage that was used for the reaffirmation and legitimizing of several heterogeneous identities that existed in the dancehall dis/place. The ongoing dialogue between the onstage dancehall artistes and the offstage audience was one key element in this process. As the night progressed, the unfolding events at Sting 1991 were perceived by the audience as overt attempts to limit or tamper with this ongoing exchange of ideas.

In similar fashion to the progression of events described earlier at Reggae Sunsplash, Sting evolved from a muted buzz of preen and pose to a deafening crescendo of screams, rag and towel salutes, shouts, gun salutes, and frenzied gyrations facing the stage. This moment, in the wee hours of the morning, set the stage for the arrival of dancehall greats and symbolized the highest point of self-affirmation and legitimization at Sting. Correspondingly, at every staging of Sting since its inception, this moment is the most tension-filled. The nerves of the audience are stretched taut, expectantly awaiting the current icons of the dancehall. At Sting 1991, however, this moment was presaged by the performance of Bunny Wailer, an internationally renowned reggae great.

An important part of the hype that surrounds well-established and internationally renowned artistes is the fact that they usually travel with their own backing band. Consequently, Bunny Wailer's performance was announced by a lengthy band change. Bunny Wailer's performance was excellent and he enjoyed an encore, yet based on my years of immersion "inna di dancehall", my own sense of the audience vibes was that, in the main, their response was one of respectful tolerance. As a reggae legend, Bunny Wailer merited his performative moment; however, on the dancehall stage and in the dancehall dis/place of the 1990s, his role was as a famous ambassador and a respected artiste from another stage and another era. He was literally out of time. The vibes flowing through the audience evidenced a general perception that the imminent arrival of the dancehall icons onstage was frozen in time and would not be animated until Bunny Wailer's performance was over and another lengthy band change had taken place. Nonetheless, the Sting audience waited long-sufferingly for his performance to end so they could resume their engagement with "their own" artistes from audience to stage and back again. For this audience, Bunny Wailer offered no mirrored symbols of socio-political engagement on the localized discourse of popular culture that spoke to the harshness of life in specific Jamaican inner-city communities such as Tivoli, Rema, Back-To, Jungle or Seaview Gardens. His identity, persona, language and style of engagement spoke to other symbols and ideologies with which the children of the dancehall – those in the Sting 1991 audience – could not or would not identify. The notions of African identity, diasporan unity, Rastafarian mythos and a more global notion of blackness, race and culture, which Louis Chude-Sokei identifies as "central to a Rastafarian Pan Africanism",[22] had been displaced by the requisite symbols of the new economic and cultural order that the dancehall represented.

At the end of his second appearance onstage, Bunny Wailer departed to the hum of approval of the dancehall audience. From my position in the audience and my countless hours spent at stage shows and similar events, it was clear that this hum of approval symbolized the audience's pregnant gratitude for the conclusion of his performance as well as an expression of the high level of anticipation for the stage entrance of their dancehall icons. However, this muted, visceral hum was misinterpreted by Bunny Wailer as a call for an encore. He proceeded to again take control of the stage, chanting his praise of some popular dancehall sound systems. At this moment, the thinly stretched nerves of the audience erupted into roars of disapproval. Notions of traditional authority and legitimacy were dis/placed within this extended and freer space of Sting 1991. Moreover, since Bunny Wailer bore the markers of another era and another group, his role in the dancehall dis/place was perceived as negligible by the Sting audience. He was disposable.

Many individuals in the Sting 1991 audience felt that the "outsider",

Bunny Wailer, had overstayed his welcome and was being both dismissive of their wishes and disrespectful towards their dancehall artistes. As a result, the Sting 1991 crowd erupted into an enraged mass. The choice viewing positions directly in front of the stage, which my group preferred, became fraught with imminent peril as one man bent to pick up a bottle and lobbed it onstage directly at Bunny Wailer. My friends and I were forced to cover our heads and duck as more glass bottles and other missiles shot towards the stage from various locations. Bunny Wailer's frantic and insistent attempts to calm the seething, frenzied mob failed and he ran off the stage as a hail of glass bottles showered down. Blood also rained down as the man crouching directly behind my friend was hit in his head. We covered our heads and tried to escape into the earth.

Suddenly, the audience's violent outburst was halted by the arrival of their icon, Ninjaman. He halted the next flood of bottles onstage as arms that were outstretched with bottles in hand halted in mid-air at the sound of his voice: "Hooold on," he insisted. Responding with roars and screams of "Ninjaaaaa!", the audience's brutal mood was instantly converted to one of joyous adulation.

Secure in his role as clashmaster, Ninjaman succeeded in sealing the ruptures within Sting 1991 as he had at Border Clash 1990. He launched into a volley of his own hits that fed the yawning hunger of the massive Sting 1991 audience. This was what the majority had journeyed from their various communities to savour. Ninjaman's charismatic performance and stage-audience treatises encapsulated the symbols and imagery that affirmed the social and political identities of the majority of the patrons at Sting 1991. This audience wanted to hear about the harsh conditions that they faced in Kingston's inner cities; they wanted to hear gun tunes and tunes of violence; they wanted to immerse themselves in the flood of dancehall stories about individuals like themselves, with similar opportunities and experiences.

This moment of highly publicized clash between two ideologically variant cultural and political spaces clearly outlined the borders of sociocultural and sociopolitical engagement in 1990s Jamaica. This clash of borders highlighted the ideological switch from the Rastafari-influenced roots rock and culture engagement of the 1970s to the new *enfant terrible* of popular culture – the dancehall. It signified a disjuncture between reggae and dancehall, its poor relative; they were related but different forms of music culture. It pointed to a radical change in the contemporary audience's respect for and response to reggae music and its mainly Rastafari-influenced ambassadors who still held their hard-won currency and esteem as cultural and music icons within and beyond the borders of Jamaica's music and culture. It showed, significantly and obviously, that the stage of the then emergent dancehall at Sting 1991 was a shifting binary scale tilted in favour of the new music genre and its adherents. This clash of borders proffered the seething and volatile nature of dancehall culture and contemporary Jamaica to the scrutiny of outsiders and hoisted aloft the more insistent, demanding, violent and modern symbols of the dancehall dis/place to public scrutiny – the hard and dangerous glass of the dark brown, imported Shandy bottle.

I want to register here the subsequent adaptations in Jamaican popular culture where the hybrid "dancehall Rasta" emerged as a necessary merger of these two co-existing strands of discourse in Jamaica. An important example is Capleton, who progressed from dancehall deejay to dancehall Rasta and pioneered the "more fire" sound and attitude associated with other dancehall Rasta artistes like Anthony B and Sizzla. The artiste lineup of Sting 2004 emphasizes this hybrid trend with an oversupply of cultural and Rasta artistes more suited to the lineup of Tony Rebel's own Rebel Salute, a Rastafari-influenced, cultural reggae event, or Morgan Heritage's newer Eastfest, than to the palpable hardcore dancehall aura that Sting projects.[23]

The blurred boundaries of performative violence in the dancehall have been analysed in the foregoing examples of Reggae Sunsplash 1989, Border Clash 1990 and Sting 1991. All these examples of violence were confined within the performative event and posed little real threat to individuals outside the dis/place. Indeed, any stage show, street dance or club in Jamaica or any other popular area in the dancehall dis/place may exhibit some combination of the volatile factors that can lead to violence. Where onstage violence between artistes is concerned, many artistes have been noted for their involvement in violent interaction both on- and offstage. Often, personal tensions brewing in the dancehall dis/place are fought out lyrically and physically at the performative event. Indeed, dancehall artiste Ninjaman has become immortalized in dancehall legend as the ultimate lyrical gladiator and clashmaster. Ninjaman's spectacular and successful lyrical *murderation* of Shabba Ranks at Sting 1990 and Supercat at Sting 1991 resulted in his being crowned the ultimate lyrical gladiator in the dancehall. At Sting 1990, Ninjaman's lyrical jibes, jabs and volleys succeeded in flustering Shabba Ranks who was rendered lyrically bankrupt onstage. Shabba Ranks lost his composure to the extent that he was reduced to tears and was forced to hastily exit the stage.

The following year at Sting 1991, the lyrical war onstage between Ninjaman and Supercat resulted in incensed supporters of Ninjaman lobbing bottles onstage, one of which hit Supercat. Supercat's fast-fading composure vanished altogether and he picked up a bottle off the stage and ferociously flung it back into the audience. He then turned to the Sting audience and threateningly informed the crowd that he had his gun with him at which point he was hastily escorted off the stage by Isaiah Laing of Supreme Promotions.

In both instances, Ninjaman triumphantly declared his lyrical prowess to the cheering and exuberant Sting crowd over the now lyrically "dead" body of his opponent. Both events remain immortalized in dancehall legend and serve to remind the dancehall body of Ninjaman's undying prowess as the ultimate lyrical gladiator, even with subsequent lyrical challenges from artistes such as Merciless and Vybz Cartel. In the early morning hours of 27 December, at Sting 2002, Ninjaman used his position as a dancehall icon and cultural griot to publicly hand over a Glock semi-automatic pistol with four bullets in its magazine to the senior superintendent of police Reneto Adams,[24] one of Jamaica's most feared crime fighters and the then head of the Crime Management Unit, an elite unit set up within the Jamaica Constabulary Force to deal with the over-whelming levels of violent crime that plague Jamaica. I also wish to note the subsequent year's debacle between Ninjaman and Vybz Kartel at Sting 2003, where their lyrical clash ended in a brawl onstage.[25]

As the ultimate clashmaster, Ninjaman's use and endorsement of an extreme, ritualized, aggressive and violent masculinity reflects and maintains the status quo. It panders to and supports the masculine tenets that form the foundation of the hegemonic structures which underpin social, political and economic life in Jamaican society. For lower-class, working-

DJ Charlie Chaplin (centre) *acts as peacemaker and gets DJs Ninjaman* (right) *and Shabba Ranks* (left) *to shake hands onstage at the end of their long-awaited lyrical clash that almost turned ugly. Courtesy of the Gleaner Company Limited.*

class and inner-city men in Jamaica, aggression, forcefulness, violence and phallic imagery become even more important markers of their masculine status as they negotiate the treacherous spaces between their marginalized lives and the hegemonic images of masculinity. The dons, shottas and clashmasters are lyrical, symbolic and real men who embody different and related manifestations of an identity that is founded on violence.

Consequently, linkages between lyrical violence and real violence are more particularly evident when one examines the harsh sociopolitical and economic realities of the inner cities, which impact directly on the creation of symbols and ideologies that are encoded in the output of the dancehall. The violent outbursts in the dancehall dis/place remain confined within the performative moment and among actors in this arena. From the clashes between sound systems to the clashes between artistes to the clashes between the artistes and the audience, the real and lyrical violence of the dancehall remain confined within the dis/place. The only real moment of violent interaction between the state and the dis/place is often catalysed by the activities of members of the Jamaica Constabulary Force, whose intervention usually succeeds in "mashing up di dance" (breaking up the dance). This is described in Buju Banton's "Operation Ardent" in graphic detail. Buju talks about a security force raid of a dance and their use of "helicopter inna air and bright light a shine a grung" (a flying helicopter with bright lights shining down on the ground), which makes him "decide fi run, cause mi nuh want nuh frisk dung" (decide to run, because I don't want to be frisked). The comedic image that Buju describes of "man a try squeeze knife dung inna Red Stripe beer" (a man trying to squeeze a knife into a bottle of Red Stripe beer) is shadowed by the more sinister promise of the threat of arrest and charges that these security officers pose to members of the dancehall massive who may be caught with weapons or illegal drugs.

In the context of state intervention, the Noise Abatement Act 1997 (often refered to as the Night Noise Act or Night Noise Law) has provided the Jamaica Constabulary Force with state-sanctioned ammunition and authority over the performative activities of the dancehall dis/place. The act stipulates that at two o'clock in the morning a sound system should be inaudible at a distance of one hundred metres. Further, it states that promoters must apply to the police at least ten days before the date for permission to host events. This has created many tensions in the dancehall dis/place and has served to further ignite the already tense relations between the state and the dis/place.[26] In addition, the consistent labelling by actors in the broader social space of socially inflammatory or sexually explicit discourse from the dancehall as "not fit for airplay" has served to demonize, delegitimize and delimit the scope of dancehall discourses within the wider society. However, within the spaces of the dancehall dis/place and in the group of dancehall adherents, these discourses maintain their potency.

Wi versus Dem

The role of the lyrical and real violence in the dancehall dis/place remains problematic in Jamaica as members of "decent" Jamaican society insist that the messengers of violence (the don daddas, the don gorgons, the colonels, the clashmasters, the warlords and the shottas) from the dis/place are the main contributors to the increase in violent crime. Although Jamaica continues to suffer high levels of violent crime, this argument is not supported by any scientific research or statistics.

Therefore, the underlying lyrical and symbolic threats of violence in the dancehall remain controversial for many middle-, upper- and lower-class Jamaicans who classify themselves as "decent" citizens in direct opposition to the "vulgar" and indecent masses who comprise the dancehall adherents. The problematic and moral panic is, however, heightened when the class ambivalence that is a part of comtemporary Jamaica is coupled with a genuine interest in dancehall music and culture. This convergence encourages individuals from the different class configurations to vacillate in their efforts to self-identify as either *wi* or *dem* based on the output of the dancehall. In the framework of inflammatory lyrics that privilege badman or shotta status as a valid identity, those who identify with the *wi* would be identified as deviant ghetto people, illegal gunmen and criminals who deserve to be shot down in the streets by police. On the other hand, those who fall in the *dem* category, would be identified as "good people", decent citizens who are constantly at risk of falling prey to these merciless gunmen, these criminals. To identify with either category is fraught with negativity. In the first instance, one would be at risk of sanctions by the state, and in the second, at risk of attack by gun-toting criminals. The most preffered response to this ideological dilemma has been to censor the public airing of these lyrical treatises. Songs like Bounty Killer's "Cyaan Believe Mi Eyes", "Look, Anytime" and "If a Warlord Did Rule di World", Baby Cham's "Mr Babylon Bwoy", and their duet, "Another Level" represent elements of the new, revolutionary use of violence encoding the *wi* versus *dem* discourse.

Identity Politics inna the Belly of the Dancehall

DANCEHALL CULTURE OPERATES in a marginalized dis/place within which actors strive to create and re-present their own identity. The dis/place as a physical and ideological space and a site of sociopolitical interaction is central to these narratives and negotiations where the dancehall dis/place acts as a popular cultural site of interrogation, contestation and meaning-making for its affectors and affectees.

The language of the dancehall dis/place is Jamaican creole or patois (*patwa*). This creolized mix of African retentions and British English has historically been the language of the Jamaican masses. The media and other new technologies that capture and disseminate dancehall lyrics and culture ensure that this is the language that is recorded and circulated locally, regionally and internationally among dancehall adherents. The historical negation of this African creolized language as a part of the dominant Eurocentric ethos that favours British English enhances the creation of an imagined community of Jamaicans at home and in the diaspora through a common, natal language. Dancehall's reliance on patois and inner-city slang effectively creates a popular cultural state that rivals the existing state structures.[1]

The dancehall also provides a vibrant economic base that guarantees economic mobility to many in the informal sector and this economic and social mobility tampers with the traditionally prescribed and often inaccessible or empty routes of education, professional standing and nepotism. Indeed, dancehall music and culture is organically tied to inner-city youths and the dis/placed masses. Its musical treatises offer a ray of hope for many who may aspire to careers in entertainment or the informal, entrepreneurial sector. When one examines the luxurious lifestyles of dancehall stars, it is obvious that careers in the dancehall earn enormous fortunes for many individuals engaged in its creation, promotion or dissemination. Additionally, the dancehall is extremely entertaining and provides an arena for its adherents to let off steam and "level the vibes". It has been argued that the release occasioned for many at a dancehall event is valuable to society as a whole because, as some oppressed youths claim, without its catharsis they may be forced to "clean their machines" (fire their guns), commit criminal acts or let off steam on the society.[2]

Where sexuality and gender is concerned, the narratives of the dancehall dis/place are actively foregrounding and repositioning extreme discourses of feminine and masculine play. These discourses position female sexuality as both a tradeable commodity and a tool that can empower women. Yet they simultaneously place the female body in a rigid space of male dominance and articulate narratives on, within and over the female body to generate masculine upliftment. Dancehall's gendered and sexual discourses play with, against and into the hegemonic patriarchal structures by legitimizing the heterosexuality and promiscuity of men while simultaneously denouncing male homosexuality.

These factors and themes in the dancehall dis/place emanate from and focus around sociopolitical issues of identity, legitimacy and freedom. Actors in the dancehall are engaged in a battle for space which encapsulates the creation and re-presentation of identities and the dissemination and consumption of symbols of real and personal power and freedom within the imagined community of dancehall's cultural space – the space that extends beyond Jamaica's geographical borders in an "imagined cultural community". In this community, actors strive to maintain and enjoy ideological, social, economic and political freedom within a marginalized dis/place that has consistently denied them freedom from as far back as the slavery era through to colonialism, neo-colonialism and

beyond. The poor, black individual has remained poor and black, existing at the very base of Jamaican society.

An in-depth sociological study on the shifts in the composition of the
Jamaican middle classes is long overdue. Nonetheless, my own work in
the dancehall confirms that the shifts occasioned by the entrepreneurial
ethos of members of the predominantly black lower class has created an
opposing pole for class identity and promotes the continued slippage of
Jamaica's traditionally rigid class structure. No longer are Jamaicans
only gaining economic and material resources through the accepted and
prescribed routes, because money has become one of the main determi-
nants of class status, coupled with one's ability to live a lifestyle closely
approximating North American ideals.[3] Carl Stone's work more than
two decades ago on Jamaica's class structure confirmed this focus on
economic wealth as an indicator of class status, but only in a context
where the wealthy also bore other markers of middle-class status.[4]
Economic capital was tightly bound to educational and cultural capital.
In contradiction, the accepted markers of middle-class status – education, white-collar profession, social background, "accepted" social
behaviour and lighter skin colour were and are conspicuously absent
from the new group of economically mobile citizens (ICIs, artistes and
drug dons, for example). The visibility and pervasiveness of this new
group tampers with the accepted notions of self and personhood in
Jamaica.

Consequently, as status, respectability and legitimacy in Jamaica
become increasingly defined by the acquisition and conspicuous consumption of more and more symbols of wealth, the most prominent and
visible creators and disseminators of the flashy dancehall culture and
hype (such as the deejays, dancers or models) are elevated to the status
of role models. The once traditional and socially accepted career paths
of lawyer, doctor or teacher are fast becoming obsolete as a route to
mobility and many young people from various socioeconomic backgrounds now view careers in the dancehall as deejays or promoters as
accessible, positive and rewarding options.

In this environment, dancehall culture supports and legitimizes the
use of wealth and/or money as a determinant of status in society. In the
dancehall dis/place, economic wealth is translated into power and

respectability. This corresponds with Stone's earlier work on class, status and mobility in Jamaica. The dancehall actor who can flaunt his or her wealth by conspicuous consumption of material resources is accorded high levels of respect and much honour.[5] Yet the strong colonial ethos that continues to undergird Jamaican society means that even with their economic wealth, brand-name clothing, luxurious cars and suburban homes, many dancehall actors are denied accession to the real middle-class identity and attendant social status and prestige that their economic wealth should bestow. The unfailing efforts to demonize and infantilize the output of the dancehall, labelling it as a trivial, temporary and vulgar offshoot of so-called pure reggae music is a part of the ethos to keep dancehall stunted and paralysed, lest Jamaica become overtaken by the buggu-yagga mores of ghetto people. In fact, like its Rastafari-influenced predecessor, dancehall music and culture has suffered from a scarcity of accessible research and documented analysis by Jamaica's premier seat of higher learning, the University of the West Indies. Identity and Conduct in Dancehall Culture, the single course on the the university's curriculum that examines dancehall, was introduced in the Faculty of Social Sciences in the 2002–2003 academic year by Dr Kingsley Stewart, a Jamaican anthropologist educated in the United States. Additionally, hardcore dancehall events like Sting still suffer from a lack of adequate sponsorship, when compared to other elite events like Jamaica Carnival, which was imported into Jamaica in 1989 by the brown-skinned elites.

The actual impact of dancehall culture on the society is best measured by first analysing its effect on those who create, disseminate, consume and exist within this cultural dis/place, that is, the affectors and affectees. Given that dancehall is a cultural phenomenon, its actors and creators are also consumers, and vice versa. The response of members of traditional society to dancehall culture is catalytic, since their frantic attempts to negate the dancehall dis/place open the door for a dialogue that confirms its incipient threat to the traditional sites of power. Their efforts to reorient, stifle or censor the manifestations that emanate from this constrained dis/place actually ensure the perpetual redefinition and rebirth, together with the continued existence, of dancehall culture.

The Politics of Appearance: Identity and Re-presentation Inna de Dancehall Dis/place

Physical appearance remains one of the most crucial factors underlying sociopolitical interaction in Jamaica. The linkages between physical appearance on the one hand and social constructs of class, colour and gendered identities on the other are far-reaching. Self re-presentation in this framework is loaded with historical, material, symbolic and class identity meanings. In the dancehall dis/place, the body is the ultimate cultural capital. It is a representative canvas that is adorned and access-orized with regalia (clothing, jewellery, hairstyles and hair colours) which portray a heterogeneous range of symbols that have become asso-ciated with a dancehall and inner-city identity. This identity is daring, aggressive, loud and demanding, and it is ostensibly identified with the dark-skinned, "lower orders" of Jamaica.

The politics of identity re-presentation operates on two levels both within and beyond the dancehall dis/place. Individuals who identify with the values and attitudes of the dancehall dis/place use physical markers of dress, hairstyle and speech to identify members of their group. These markers are parodied and performed within dancehall and inner-city cul-ture. Positive identification of a member of this group results in the camaraderie and open communication that legitimizes this dancehall identity. Individuals who are neither of nor from this group often react negatively to persons whose physical markers, attitudes and style of dress identify them as a part of the dis/place. This dialogue is often marred by confrontation, dismissal or outright disrespect. For example, a woman who wears elaborate hairstyles, dresses in flashy, revealing costumes and sports large amounts of gold jewellery is usually referred to as wearing "dancehall style" even if she is not seen at a dancehall event. "Those dancehall people" is a commonly used phrase, particularly when the dancehall is being demonized or infantilized. In fact, during my pre-aca-demic years of employment in corporate Jamaica, I was taken to task by a concerned colleague of mine who felt that I was too intellectually supe-rior to be involved with "those dancehall people down there". She felt that my time would be better served doing something more intellectually and morally uplifting than mixing "those ghetto people".

Women in dancehall regalia arrive at Bogle's funeral, Kencot Seventh Day Adventist Church, Kingston, March 2005. Donna P. Hope photo.

Dancehall's emphasis on costuming and public performance is organically linked to the development of what I call the "video-light syndrome" in the dancehall dis/place. This powerful need to be seen, documented, photographed and, in particular, videotaped, has been an important part of dancehall culture since the introduction of video cameras as a regular part of activities in the dancehall in the late 1980s to early 1990s.[6] The rise of Jamaica's local cable television industry at around this time also contributed to this phenomenon, as local cable providers film sections of dancehall events and broadcast them on their local cable channels. The video-light syndrome refers to the insatiable desire of many dancehall patrons to have their presence documented at the dances, stage shows and other dancehall events that they attend. Many of these individuals will go to great lengths to ensure that their images are captured on camera. This includes wearing elaborate and expensive jewellery and regalia; conspicuous purchase and consumption of expensive, brand-name beverages such as Moet & Chandon and Alizé; along with wearing revealing clothes and the performance of

Dancers at the weekly hype dancehall event Passa Passa Wednesdays pose in front of Miles Enterprises on Spanish Town Road, December 2004. Roy Sweetland photo.

erotic, X-rated dances by women. With the recent explosion of male dancers in the dancehall, pioneered by the late master dancer Bogle (Gerald Levy), female dancers are now forced to share the dancing stage with their male counterparts. Dancehall events provide central spaces for the presentation of self and status in the dis/place because the now common fixture of cameras promises considerable rewards in terms of visibility, recognition, status and sometimes real resources to those whose images are captured while in action at these events. Accordingly, dancehall stage shows and popular events, such as the weekly event Passa Passa[7] and the funerals of prominent affectors such as Willie Haggart in 2001 and Bogle in 2005,[8] provide a multifaceted, theatrical stage on which the marginalized children of the poverty-stricken inner cities of Kingston, St Andrew and St Catherine can *bruk 'way* and indulge in frenetic, spiritual rituals of self-affirmation and renewal. In a critical moment of self-affirmation that bestows social and cultural empowerment, the dancers, profilers modellers, queens and other adherents of the dancehall proclaim their existence and declare that "wi a smaddy too" (We too are individuals of merit). The children of the dancehall and inner city fight frenetically for their tiny bit of space so that their images may be conveyed elsewhere by digital video signals, because they are sensitized to the empowering potential of the cameras to liberate their fractured images from the social and political entrapment in the poverty-stricken inner cities of Kingston. The multiplicity of dancehall images implode in the dis/place where African retentions, creolized dance and inner-city style merge with high technology "pon di river pon di bank" and explode outwards through the eyelights, highlights, floodlights of the cameras. Even if it is for a moment, these adherents of the dancehall are freed, seen and heard. They transcend their confining identities and become popularized as the kings, queens and superstars of the dancehall.

The problematic narratives of identity renegotiation, transformation and re-presentation in the dis/place articulate the social tensions and the ongoing transformation in the traditional social hierarchy. The *wi* versus *dem* exchange that is now a strident part of the ongoing discourse of the dis/place encodes both a mindless dalliance, with extremes of violence or raw sexuality, and more importantly, an attempt to use this discourse as a vehicle for attaining legitimacy and freedom. The perceived threat of this *wi* versus *dem* arises because the increasingly violated and violent majority amplify their social, political and economic frustrations through the cultural vehicle of the dis/place: dancehall music. Since this music and the cultural symbols of the dis/place continue to enjoy high levels of public broadcast, locally and internationally, then the inherent tensions of the *wi* versus *dem* dialogue escalates proportionately. This discourse serves a revolutionary purpose in awakening and developing identities and sites of power that are not oriented around traditional prescribed sites. The problematic is grounded in the increasing polarization of groups in the society on a stage where the battle for social and political space is ongoing. This is amplified, since the narrative dialogue of the dancehall emanates from the lower orders and is couched in the overtly threatening tones of messengers with lower-class and inner-city origins, and whose class aspiration is blurred. Dancehall culture becomes a true site of contestation as different groups jockey for hierarchical positions in a rigid, class-structured society.

Dancehall culture's dialogue of extreme violence and crass, vulgar sexualities disturbs the peace of traditional Jamaica because it represents a viable alternative and a contending power that rivals the dominance of the traditional bourgeois class. Nevertheless, in its greatest moment of revolution, the dancehall dis/place also draws from its surroundings and ultimately replicates the tensions and contradictions of the patriarchal structures that are at work in Jamaica.

Notes

Chapter 1

1. John D. Forbes, *Jamaica: Managing Political and Economic Change* (Washington, DC: American Enterprise Institute for Public Policy Research, 1985), 10.
2. Ibid., 11.
3. Evelyne Huber Stephens and John D. Stephens, *Democratic Socialism in Jamaica: The Political Movement and Social Transformation in Dependent Capitalism* (London: Macmillan, 1986), 150.
4. Ibid.; Derick Boyd, *Economic Management, Income Distribution, and Poverty in Jamaica* (New York: Praeger, 1988).
5. Boyd, *Economic Management*, 26.
6. Stephanie Black's documentary film *Life and Debt* graphically illustrates the devastating economic and political consequences of globalization and the policies of the IMF, World Bank and the Inter-American Development Bank on a developing country like Jamaica.
7. Michael Manley details this experience in his book *Jamaica: Struggle in the Periphery* (London: Third World Media, 1982). Unconfirmed reports claim one thousand deaths during that election year.
8. Patrick A.M. Emmanuel, *Elections and Party Systems in the Commonwealth Caribbean: 1944–1991* (St Michael, Barbados: Caribbean Development Research Services, 1992), 50–51.
9. Carl Stone, *Democracy and Clientelism in Jamaica* (New Brunswick, NJ: Transaction Books, 1980), 91–110. Stone examines this phenomenon in depth in his chapter "Clientelism, Power and Democracy".
10. Ibid., 91–92.
11. Ibid., 101.
12. Ibid., 100.
13. Quoted in "Report of the National Committee on Political Tribalism" (1997), 7.

14. For an in-depth discussion on these communities see Christopher Charles, "Garrison Politics", *Jamaica Herald,* 29 May 1996, and "Garrison Communities as Counter Societies: The Case of the 1998 Zeeks' Riot in Jamaica", *Ideaz* 1 (2002): 29–43. Also see Mark Figueroa and Amanda Sives, "Homogeneous Voting, Electoral Manipulation and the 'Garrison' Process in Post-independence Jamaica", *Journal of Commonwealth and Comparative Politics* 40 (2002); as well as "Report of the National Committee on Political Tribalism" (1997).

15. Derek Gordon, Patricia Anderson and Don Robotham, "Jamaica: Urbanization during the Years of Crisis", in *The Urban Caribbean: Transition to the New Global Economy,* ed. Alejandro Portes, Carlos Dobre-Cabral and Patricia Landolt (Baltimore: Johns Hopkins University Press, 1997), 190–223.

16. Forbes, *Jamaica,* 27, 36.

17. Boyd, *Economic Management,* 53, 58.

18. Elsie Le Franc, ed., *Consequences of Structural Adjustment: A Review of the Jamaican Experience* (Kingston: Canoe Press, 1994), 42.

19. The parish of Kingston is classified as 100 per cent urban in Jamaica's national censuses of 1982 and 1991. This is followed by the parishes of St Andrew with 87 per cent and St Catherine with 70.7 per cent.

20. One segment of Black's *Life and Debt* focuses on Jamaica's free trade zones where mainly female workers toiled sewing garments for American manufacturers five or six days per week in near-sweatshop conditions for the then legal minimum wage of US$30 a week. No unionization is permitted in these foreign-owned garment factories where shiploads of material arrive tax-free for assembly by Jamaican workers before being transported back to foreign markets. The first free zone, the Kingston Free Zone, was created in 1976 on ground adjacent to the Kingston Container Terminal. The eighteen-hectare site contains 72,835 square metres of factory space. The other major free zones are Montego Bay Free Zone, Garmex Free Zone, Hayes Free Zone and Cazoumar Free Zone. From 1985 to 1995, the combined export output in textiles of the zones was US$1.31 billion. Around twelve thousand people were employed in the textile factories, about 1.6 per cent of the total workforce. However, since 1995 the industry has been in a serious depression due to structural problems in Jamaica and increased foreign competition. See "Jamaican Free Zones", *Fact Index,* http://www.fact-index.com/j/ja/jamaican_free_zones.html.

21. Gordon, Anderson and Robotham, "Jamaica".
22. Statistical Institute of Jamaica, "Population Census 2001", http://www.statinja.com/census.html.
23. Statistical Institute of Jamaica, "The Labour Force" (typescript, 1985).
24. Kari Polanyi Levitt, *The Origins and Consequences of Jamaica's Debt Crisis, 1970–1990,* rev. ed. (Kingston: Consortium Graduate School of Social Sciences, University of the West Indies, 1991), 48, table 16.
25. Ibid., 45, table 14.
26. Planning Institute of Jamaica, *Estimates of Poverty in Jamaica for the Years 1992 and 1993* (Kingston: Planning Institute of Jamaica, 1994), 15–16.
27. Anita Waters, *Race, Class and Political Symbols: Rastafari and Reggae in Jamaican Politics* (New Brunswick, NJ: Transaction Books, 1985), 26.
28. See Carl Stone, *Class, Race and Political Behaviour in Urban Jamaica* (Kingston: Institute of Social and Economic Research, University of the West Indies, 1973), as well as his *Class, State, and Democracy in Jamaica* (New York: Praeger, 1986) and *Democracy and Clientelism.*
29. Stone, *Democracy and Clientelism,* 20–21.
30. Keith Hart, "Informal Income Opportunities and Urban Employment in Ghana", *Journal of Modern African Studies* 11 (1973): 61–89.
31. Alejandro Portes, Manuel Castells and Lauren A. Benton, eds., *The Informal Economy: Studies in Advanced and Less Developed Countries* (Baltimore: Johns Hopkins University Press, 1989).
32. Ibid.
33. Elsie Le Franc, "Petty Trading and Labour Mobility: Higglers in the Kingston Metropolitan Area", in *Caribbean Sociology: Introductory Readings,* ed. Christine Barrow and Rhoda Reddock (Kingston: Ian Randle, 2001), 801–23.
34. Ibid., 808.
35. Edward Brathwaite, *The Development of Creole Society in Jamaica 1770–1820* (Oxford: Clarendon Press, 1971), 297.
36. Rex Nettleford, *Caribbean Cultural Identity: The Case of Jamaica: An Essay on Cultural Dynamics* (Los Angeles: UCLA Latin American Center Publications, 1979).
37. Erna Brodber, "Socio-Cultural Change in Jamaica", in *Jamaica in Independence,* ed. Rex Nettleford (Kingston: Heinemann Caribbean, 1989), 54–74.

38. Mervyn C. Alleyne, *The Construction and Representation of Race and Ethnicity in the Caribbean* (Kingston: University of the West Indies Press, 2001).

39. See the discussion on the Jamaican political economy in Stone, *Class, State, and Democracy,* 28–47, and in particular his discussion of this petty commodity sector on p. 36.

40. See Norman Stolzoff, *Wake the Town and Tell the People: Dancehall Culture in Jamaica* (Durham: Duke University Press, 2000), 105; Colin Larkin, *The Virgin Encyclopaedia of Reggae* (London: Virgin Books, 1998), 322–23.

41. Kevin O'Brien Chang and Wayne Chen, *Reggae Routes: The Story of Jamaican Music* (Kingston: Ian Randle, 1998), 68–69.

42. Steve Barrow and Peter Dalton, *Reggae: The Rough Guide* (London: Rough Guides, 1997), 18–19, 114–17.

43. Larkin, *The Virgin Encyclopedia, 304–5.*

44. Dick Hebdige, *Cut n' Mix: Culture, Identity and Caribbean Music* (London: Methuen, 1987), 24.

45. For her discussion and analysis of this phenomenon see Carolyn Cooper, *Sound Clash: Jamaican Dancehall Culture at Large* (New York: Palgrave Macmillan, 2004). In particular, see her chapter " 'More Fire': Chanting Down Babylon from Bob Marley to Capleton", 179–206.

46. For an intense analysis of the role of sound system culture on the development of dancehall music and culture, see Stolzoff, *Wake the Town.*

47. See Market Research Services, "Jamaica Media Survey" (report, 1991), 2, and "All Media Survey" (report, 1995), 1.

48. These radio stations are as follows: Irie FM; Love 101; Linkz 96 FM; RJR 94 FM; MegaJamz; Radio Mona; Kool 97 FM; Hot 102 FM; Mello FM 96; Klas FM; Fame 95 FM, Radio 2; Zip 103 FM; 99 Music FM; and Power 106 FM.

49. From author's content analysis of programme content for these two stations.

50. See, for example, letters to the editor from veteran journalist Fae Ellington, *Jamaica Gleaner,* 7 August 2001, and secretary of the Jamaica Federation of Musicians Carl Ayton, *Jamaica Gleaner,* 18 August 1987; and articles by Clifton Segree, "Put Some Decency into Dancehall Dress", *Jamaica Gleaner,* 27 February 2000, and Dawn Johnson, "Who Wants to Listen to Crap?", *Jamaica Gleaner,* 5 September 1999.

51. See, for example, Andrew Clunis, "Music Polluting Young Minds", *Jamaica Gleaner*, 7 May 2000; Richard Morais, "Popular Culture Blamed for Boys' Poor Grades", *Jamaica Gleaner*, 21 January 2000; Barbara Nelson, "The Church Speaks on Vulgar Lyrics and Gun Violence", *Sunday Gleaner*, 30 January 1994; "Views from the West: Would the Imposing of a Ban on Dancehall Music Reduce Crime in Jamaica?", *Jamaica Gleaner*, 18 May 2000; Howard Campbell, "PM Appeals for End to Gun Lyrics", *Jamaica Observer*, 12 August 1999.

52. See, for example, Ayton, letter to the editor; Headley H.G. Jones (president of the Jamaica Federation of Musicians), letter to the editor, *Jamaica Gleaner*, 19 August 1989; Nelson, "The Church Speaks"; Hedley H.G. Jones, "Our Musical Heritage", *Sunday Gleaner*, 16 October 1994; Ian Burrell, "A Shift in Reggae Consciousness?", *Sunday Herald*, 20 November 1994.

53. See Paul Gilroy, *There Ain't no Black in the Union Jack: The Cultural Politics of Race and Nation* (London: Routledge, 1995); Hebdige, *Cut n' Mix*.

54. See Carolyn Cooper's feminist-influenced treatise on the dancehall in "Erotic Play in the Dance Hall", parts 1 and 2, *Jamaica Journal* 22 no. 4 and 23 no. 1 (1990), and the chapter "Slackness Hiding from Culture: Erotic Play in the Dancehall" in her book *Noises in the Blood: Orality, Gender, and the "Vulgar" Body of Jamaican Popular Culture*, Warwick University Caribbean Studies Series (London: Macmillan, 1993), 136–73.

55. Sylvester Ayre, letter to the editor, *Jamaica Gleaner*, 14 March 2000; Ayton, letter to the editor; Ian Boyne, "Decadent Dancehall Mirrors Society", *Sunday Gleaner*, 5 January 1997; Burrell, "A Shift"; Andrew Clunis, "Reggae Music Suffering Because of Violence", *Star* (Jamaica), 6 May 1999; Clunis, "To the Bin with Filthy Lyrics" *Jamaica Gleaner*, 27 August 1999; Clunis, "Music Polluting"; Donna Hope, "Sting 2003: Performing Violence and Social Commentary", *Sunday Gleaner*, 4 January 2004; Jones, letter to the editor; Morais, "Popular Culture"; Nelson, "The Church Speaks"; Clifton Segree, "Too Much Disposable Music", *Jamaica Gleaner*, 9 February 2000; Segree, "Put Some Decency"; Claude Wilson, "Mobay Artiste Stokes 'Shotta' Controversy", *Jamaica Gleaner*, 8 August 1999.

56. Jarrett Brown, "Masculinity and Dancehall", *Caribbean Quarterly* 45, no. 1 (March 1999): 1–16; Donna P. Hope, "Inna di Dancehall Dis/Place:

Sociocultural Politics of Identity in Jamaica" (MPhil thesis, University of the West Indies, Mona, 2001); Hope, "Sting 2003"; Hope, "The British Link-Up Crew: Consumption Masquerading as Masculinity in the Dancehall" *Interventions: International Journal of Postcolonial Studies* 6, no. 1 (April 2004): 101–17; Hope, "Clash: Gays vs. Dancehall", parts 1 and 2, *Jamaica Gleaner,* 5–6 October 2004; Keisha Lindsay, "Dance Hall Music: Political Subversion and the Rise of the Ghetto" (BA thesis, Amherst College, 1992); Norman Stolzoff, "Murderation: The Question of Violence in the Sound System Dance", *Social and Economic Studies* 47, no. 1 (March 1998); Stolzoff, *Wake the Town*; Patricia J. Saunders, "Is Not Everything Good to Eat, Good to Talk: Sexual Economy and Dancehall Music in the Global Marketplace", *Small Axe,* no. 13 (March 2003): 95–115; Imani Tafari, "Lady Saw . . . Dancehall Donette" *Sistren* 16, nos. 1–2 (1994).

57. Cooper, *Noises in the Blood,* 141.

58. Ibid., 41.

59. For a useful synopsis of these linkages, see the films *Dancehall Queen* (1997) and *Third World Cop* (2000), both produced by Island Films and the DVD release *Shottas* (2002)

60. *Bashment* and *bling bling* are hip-hop influenced words as well as inner-city slang. Both define the conspicuous, materialistic and consumptive hype of the dancehall. They are often used to refer to style of dress or the behaviour of an individual or group. Further, they are used to describe events or material goods that are either very expensive or highly rated on the hierarchy of dancehall hype. "Bling bling" is used more often with regard to material goods, while "bashment" is used more often to describe an event or a type of behaviour.

61. Lloyd Bradley, *Bass Culture: When Reggae Was King* (London: Viking, 2000); Chris Potash, ed., *Reggae, Rasta, Revolution: Jamaican Music from Ska to Dub* (New York: Schirmer Books, 1997).

62. Stuart Hall, "What Is 'Black' in Black Popular Culture?", in *Stuart Hall: Critical Dialogues in Cultural Studies,* ed. David Morley and Kuan-Hsing Chen (New York and London: Routledge, 1996), 466.

63. Ibid., 465.

64. Michael Witter, "Music and the Jamaican Economy" (report prepared for UNCTAD/WIPO, February 2002), 32–33.

65. Stolzoff, *Wake the Town,* 1.

Chapter 2

1. Hall, "What Is 'Black' ", 474.
2. In his watershed work on Jamaican dancehall culture, *Wake the Town*, Stolzoff's own typologies of dancehall deejays and singers replicate the tendency to define and identify dancehall through the activities of its most prominent actors, the artistes. See pages 163–72 of for these categories.

Chapter 3

1. For works on the social construction of gender and sexuality see, for example, Judith Butler, *Gender Trouble: Feminism and the Subversion of Identity* (London: Routledge, 1990); Michel Foucault, *The History of Sexuality: An Introduction,* volume 1 (London: Vintage, 1990); and Joan Scott, *Gender and the Politics of History* (New York: Columbia University Press, 1988), especially "Gender a Useful Category of Historical Analysis", 28–50.
2. Sandra Lipsitz Bem, *The Lenses of Gender* (New Haven: Yale University Press, 1993), 2.
3. Scott, *Gender,* 28–50.
4. Kenneth Clatterbaugh, *Contemporary Perspectives on Masculinity* (Boulder: Westview, 1997); R.W. Connell, *Gender and Power: Society, the Person and Sexual Politics* (Cambridge: Polity Press, 1987); R.W. Connell, *Masculinities* (Berkeley: University of California Press, 1995); Linden Lewis, ed., *The Culture of Gender and Sexuality in the Caribbean* (Gainesville: University Press of Florida, 2003); Stephen Whitehead and Frank J. Barrett, eds., *The Masculinities Reader* (Cambridge and Oxford: Polity and Blackwell, 2001).
5. M. Jacqui Alexander, "Not Just (Any) *Body* Can Be a Citizen: The Politics of Law, Sexuality and Postcoloniality in Trinidad and Tobago and the Bahamas", *Feminist Review* 48 (Autumn 1994) 5–23; Christine Barrow, ed., *Caribbean Portraits: Essays on Gender Ideologies and Identities* (Kingston: Ian Randle, 1998); Eudine Barriteau, "Postmodernist Feminist Theorizing and Development Policy and Practice in the Anglophone Caribbean: The Barbados Case", in *Feminism/Post-modernism/Development,* ed. Marianne Marchand and Jane Plupart

(London: Routledge, 1995); Eudine Barriteau, "Theorizing Gender
Systems and the Project of Modernity in the Twentieth Century
Caribbean", *Feminist Review* 59 (Summer 1998): 186–209; Eudine
Barriteau, *The Political Economy of Gender in the Twentieth Century
Caribbean* (Basingstoke: Palgrave, 2001); Hilary Beckles, "Sex and
Gender in the Historiography of Caribbean Slavery", in *Engendering
History: Caribbean Women in Historical Perspective,* ed. Bridget
Brereton, Barbara Bailey and Verene Shepherd (New York: St Martin's
Press, 1995), 125–38; Hilary Beckles, *Centering Woman: Gender
Discourses in Caribbean Slave Society* (Kingston: Ian Randle, 1999);
Lewis, *The Culture of Gender*; Patricia Mohammed, "From Laventille to
St Ann's: Towards a Caribbean Feminist Philosophy", *Newsletter of the
Caribbean Association for Feminist Research and Action* (1990); Patricia
Mohammed, "Nuancing the Feminist Discourse in the Caribbean", in
"New Currents in Caribbean Thought", special issue, *Social and
Economic Studies* 43, no. 3 (1994); Patricia Mohammed, "Writing
Gender into History: The Negotiation of Gender Relations", in
Engendering History: Caribbean Women in Historical Perspective, ed.
Bridget Brereton, Verene Shepherd and Barbara Bailey (Kingston: Ian
Randle, 1995), 20–47; Patricia Mohammed, ed., "Rethinking Caribbean
Difference", special issue, *Feminist Review* 59 (Summer 1998); Rhoda
Reddock, "Primacy of Gender in Race and Class", in *Race, Class and
Gender in the Future of the Caribbean,* ed. J. Edward Greene (Kingston:
Institute of Social and Economic Research, 1993), 43–73; Rhoda
Reddock, *Women, Labour and Politics in Trinidad and Tobago: A
History* (London: Zed Books, 1994).

6. Brathwaite, *The Development of Creole Society,* 297.
7. Alexander, "Not Just (Any) *Body*", 11–12.
8. For example, in *Black Feminist Thought* (New York: Routledge, 1991),
   Patricia Hill Collins discusses the inseparability of the systems of race,
   gender and class in the lives of black women in the United States.
9. M.G. Smith, *Culture, Race and Class in the Commonwealth Caribbean*
   (Kingston: Department of Extramural Studies, University of the West
   Indies, 1984).
10. The patent colour bias towards lighter-skinned women in the beauty
    contests is often debated in the electronic and print media. See, for
    example, "Beauty Contests 'Insult to Blacks' " and "The Miss Jamaica

Show", letters to the editor, *Jamaica Gleaner,* 20 September 1999; K.O. Chang, "Out of Many One Propaganda?", *Jamaica Observer,* 16 September 2002; and M. Cooke, " 'International' Standards of Beauty", *Jamaica Gleaner,* 30 August 2002.

11. Ronald Hall, "The Bleaching Syndrome: African American's Response to Cultural Domination Vis-à-Vis Skin Color", *Journal of Black Studies* 26 (1995): 172–84.

12. "Bumper" refers to the female posterior or rear end. The term is more often than not applied to those women with well-endowed, large or protruding posterior.

13. Christopher Charles, "Skin Bleaching, Self-Hate and Black Identity in Jamaica", *Journal of Black Studies* 33 (2003): 711–28.

14. David Scott, "Catching Shirt", *Small Axe,* no. 3 (1998): 115–22.

15. Charles, "Skin Bleaching".

16. Errol Miller, "Body Image, Physical Beauty and Color among Jamaican Adolescents", in *Caribbean Sociology: Introductory Readings,* ed. Rhoda Reddock and Christine Barrow (Princeton: Markus Wiener, 2001), 305–19.

17. Ibid., 317.

18 Errol Miller, *Men at Risk* (Kingston: Jamaica Publishing House, 1991).

19. Barry Chevannes, *Learning to Be a Man: Culture, Socialization and Gender Identity in Five Caribbean Communities* (Kingston: University of the West Indies Press, 2001), 202.

20. A *wukka man* refers to a man who displays skill and prowess in his sexual dealings with his women. These men are perceived as ideal sexual partners and many openly flaunt several romantic/sexual partners.

21. *Nuff gyal inna bungle* describes the multiple sexual/romantic relationships or liaisons of a traditional wukka man, a man who is perceived as attractive and powerful by women based on his sexual prowess or access to resources.

22. A *druggist* or *drug don* is a man who engages in the importation/exportation and/or dissemination of illegal narcotic drugs such as marijuana and cocaine. Though women are involved in the illegal drug trade, the term is masculine.

23. Red Dragon, *c.*1987–88.

24. Admiral Bailey's "Punaany" was voted the number one hit in the dancehall and also the wider society, based on compilations of the then JBC Radio weekly Top Forty charts.

25. See, for example, "Attack on 'Punaany' ", *Star* (Jamaica), 19 August 1988.
26. Personal Interview with male respondent, July 1998.
27. Chevannes, *Learning to Be a Man,* 140–47.
28. Ibid., 140–41.
29. Cobra, "Mate a Rebel", 1993.
30. Spragga Benz, "Girls Hoorah", 1994.
31. Based on compilations from weekly charts at the then JBC Radio.
32. "Arcade" originally refers to the Pearnel Charles Arcade in downtown Kingston named after JLP politician Pearnel Charles. The arcade was built in 1989 by the government to house the ICIs and other vendors of clothes, shoes and accessories who had overrun the streets of downtown Kingston. Another similar venue is the Constant Spring Arcade in uptown Kingston, which was built later to facilitate the explosion of ICIs above Cross Roads, which marks the boundary between uptown and downtown Kingston.
33. To "feature" in this context is to give excessive attention and/or loud accolades to an important or popular person.
34. "Older Woman, Younger Man", *Outlook Sunday Magazine,* 27 February 2005, 2–3.
35. Personal interview with key dancehall affector in March 1999.
36. *Phattest* derives from the slang *phat* which is an acronym used to refer specifically to voluptuous female sexuality focusing on specific areas of sexuality as follows: p = pussy or vagina; h = hips; a = ass and t = tits or breasts.
37. For example, see *HardCopy, Banned from HardCopy* or *XNews* newspapers.
38. *HardCopy* 3, no. 8 (18 April–1 May 2000).
39. Some of these contests were held at the then popular Cactus Nightclub in Portmore, St Catherine, which is no longer in operation. Others contests are conducted at live dancehall events. *HardCopy* features prominent write-ups and photographs of these competitions and their winners.
40. *Vibes up di place* means to increase the hype and heighten the excitement at an event. The perception that an event will be *full of vibes* encourages more patrons to attend and spend their money.
41. Jack Sowah, interview by author, Kingston, Jamaica, February 1999.
42. See Tafari, "Lady Saw"; Cooper, "Erotic Play in the Dance Hall";

Cooper, *Noises in the Blood*; Carolyn Cooper, "Punany Power", *Black Media Journal* 2 (2000): 50–52; Kezia Page, "Dancehall Feminisms: Jamaican Female Deejays and the Politics of the Big Ninja Bike" (paper presented at the conference "Borders, Boundaries and the Global in Caribbean Studies", Bowdoin College, Brunswick, Maine, 11–13 April 2003); Tracey Skelton, " 'I Sing Dirty Reality, I Am Out There for the Ladies', Lady Saw: Women and Jamaican Ragga Music, Resisting Patriarchy", *Phoebe* 7, nos. 1–2 (1995): 86–104.

43. Ibid.
44. *Battyman* is the Jamaican creole for homosexual. The word *batty* refers to one's bottom or posterior. It is then compounded with *man* to create *battyman*, where male homosexuals are defined by anal sex.
45. Examples of chi-chi man songs include: Capleton's "Bun out di Chi Chi"; TOK's "Chi Chi Man"; Elephant Man's "Log On" and Alozade's "Chi Chi Crew".
46. Chevannes, *Learning to Be a Man,* 144, 221.
47. Patrick D. Hopkins, "Gender Treachery: Homophobia, Masculinity and Threatened Identities", in *Rethinking Masculinity: Philosophical Explorations in Light of Feminism,* ed. Larry May and Robert Strikweda (Lanham, Md.: Rowman and Littlefield, 1992), 114.
48. Ibid.
49. Hope, "Inna di Dancehall", "Sting 2003", "British Link-Up Crew", and "Clash: Gays vs. Dancehall", parts 1 and 2.
50. Cecil Gutzmore, "Casting the First Stone! Policing of Homo/Sexuality in Jamaican Popular Culture", in "Jamaican Popular Culture", ed. Carolyn Cooper and Alison Donnell, special issue, *Interventions: International Journal of Postcolonial Studies* 6, no. 1 (April 2004): 126.
51. Chevannes, *Learning to Be a Man,* 144, 194, 203, 220–21.
52. For work on this debate of the local versus global in dancehall's anti-homosexual treatises, see Carolyn Cooper, "Lyrical Gun: Metaphor and Role Play in Jamaican Dancehall Culture", *Massachusetts Review* 35, nos. 3–4 (Autumn 1994): 429–47; and Saunders's "Is Not Everything Good to Eat". Cooper extends her discussion in chapter 5 of her book *Sound Clash.*
53. Gutzmore, "Casting the First Stone"; Hope "Clash: Gays vs. Dancehall", parts 1 and 2.
54. Chevannes, *Learning to Be a Man,* 221.

55. Ibid., 202–3; Hope, "Inna di Dancehall".
56. See, for example, Chevannes's work on Jamaican masculinity, *Learning to Be a Man* and *What We Sow and What We Reap: Problems in the Cultivation of Male Identity in Jamaica,* Grace, Kennedy Lecture Series (Kingston: Grace, Kennedy Foundation, 1999). For a discussion on the rigid gendering of Jamaican identities specifically see *Learning to Be a Man,* in particular 35–66, 149–204.
57. Chevannes, *Learning to Be a Man,* 220.

Chapter 4

1. Cooper, "Lyrical Gun".
2. Richard Hart, *Rise and Organise: The Birth of the Workers and National Movements in Jamaica (1936–1939)* (London: Karia Press, 1989); Ken Post, *Arise Ye Starvelings: The Jamaica Labour Rebellion of 1938 and its Aftermath* (The Hague: Martinus Nihoff, 1978); Ken Post, *Strike the Iron: A Colony at War 1939–45* (The Hague: Martinus Nihoff, 1981).
3. Human and Social Development Group, Latin America and the Caribbean Region, *Violence and Urban Poverty in Jamaica: Breaking the Cycle* (Washington, DC: World Bank, 1997), 39–42.
4. Anthony Harriott, *Police and Crime Control in Jamaica: Problems of Reforming Ex-Colonial Constabularies* (Kingston: University of the West Indies Press, 2000), 9, table 1.1.
5. Peter Phillips and Judith Wedderburn, *Crime and Violence: Causes and Solutions,* Department of Government Occasional Papers, no. 2 (Kingston: University of the West Indies, 1988), 22.
6. Bernard Headley, *The Jamaican Crime Scene: A Perspective* (Mandeville, Jamaica: Eureka Press, 1994), 24.
7. Cooper, "Lyrical Gun".
8. Barrow and Dalton, *Reggae,* 53.
9. Garth White, "Rudie, Oh Rudie", *Caribbean Quarterly* (September 1967): 39–45.
10. Barrow and Dalton, *Reggae,* 53–55.
11. Chevannes, *What We Sow,* 30.
12. From a personal interview with a dancehall affector in 2000 and my own extensive participant observation in the dancehall.

13. Charles, "Garrison Communities"; Charles Price, "What the Zeeks Uprising Reveals: Development Issues, Moral Economy and the Urban Lumpenproletariat in Jamaica", *Urban Anthropology* 33, no. 1 (Spring 2004): 73–113; see also John Rapley, "Jamaica: Negotiating Law and Order with the Dons", *NACLA Report on the Americas* 37, no. 2 (September–October 2003): 25–29.

14. Charles, "Garrison Communities", 41n1.

15. See Stone, *Democracy and Clientelism* for a discussion on the patron–clientelist structure that underpinned the Jamaican political culture and practice in the 1970s and beyond.

16. For more discussion on Jamaica's experience with structural adjustment see Le Franc, *Consequences;* Levitt, *The Origins and Consequences;* Stephens and Stephens, *Democratic Socialism.*

17. See Laurie Gunst, *Born fi' Dead: A Journey Through the Jamaican Posse Underworld* (New York: Henry Holt, 1995), for a discussion of the Jamaican underworld and its linkages to the diaspora.

18. Harriott, *Police and Crime Control,* 22.

19. Charles, "Garrison Communities", 32.

20. "Reggae Sunsplash 89", *Jamaica Gleaner,* 21 August 1989, 16.

21. The term *vibesmaster* adequately describes the role of Derek Barnett, the bass player of the Sagittarius band during the late 1980s and the early 1990s. Derek's personal, interactive style onstage (including dancing, prancing and humorous gymnastics) created an ongoing sub-narrative that enhanced the performance of the artistes. This was matched only by his musical skill and dexterity with the bass guitar.

22. Louis Chude-Sokei, "Postnationalist Geographies: Rasta, Ragga, and Reinventing Africa", in *Reggae, Rasta, Revolution: Jamaican Music from Ska to Dub,* ed. Chris Potash (New York: Schirmer Books, 1997), 216.

23. The Sting 2004 lineup included Capleton, Anthony B, Richie Spice and Jah Mason. Of the seven artistes featured as the "Magnificent Seven", six were dancehall Rastas: Mr Perfect, Ghandi, Fantan Moja, Bascom X, I Wayne and Turbulance. The seventh was Kriss Kelly, an up-and-coming female artiste. The list of hardcore dancehall artistes on Sting 2004 was conspicuously short: Beenie Man, Ninjaman, Assassin and Danny English backed up by Kiprich and the raunchy Queen Paula. This bias towards Rasta artistes and away from hardcore artistes reflected an apparent response by Sting's directors to the denunciation of violence at successive

Sting events, ending with the onstage debacle between Ninjaman and Vybz Kartel at Sting 2003. One patron of Sting 2004 remarked that Sting had "become" Rebel Salute so there was no need for patrons to attend both events. Sting 2004 had lost its sting.

24. "Ninja Man Hands Over Gun to Adams", *Jamaica Observer*, 28 December 2002, and "Adams, 'Ninja Man' Deny Gun Hand over at Sting Staged", *Jamaica Observer*, 6 January 2003.

25. See Hope, "Sting 2003", for an analysis of this event. See also Ian Boyne's commentary in " 'Sting': A Disgraced Institution", *Jamaica Gleaner*, 4 January 2004, E7–E8.

26. See, for example, " 'Tone Down, Clean Up' Cops Warn Promoters, Sound Systems", *Jamaica Gleaner*, 27 February 2000; "Sound System Operators Want Change in Noise Abatement Act", *Sunday Herald*, 14 May 2000, 1C; "Night Noises Act Drives Parties out of Town . . . and Teens in Trouble", *Jamaica Observer*, 13 August 2000, 5.

Chapter 5

1. See Cooper and Devonish's discussion of the role of language in dancehall in chapter 10, "The Dancehall Transnation", of Cooper's *Sound Clash*, 279–302.

2. Personal interviews with dancehall patrons, 1999–2003.

3. See Le Franc, *Consequences*, 59–62.

4. Stone, *Class, Race and Political Behaviour*.

5. Hope, "British Link-Up Crew".

6. Sowah, interview.

7. *Passa passa*, translated from Jamaican creole, means *mix-up* or *mix-up and blenda*, and can variously be translated to mean controversy, hullabaloo and/or nastiness. It is the name given to the popular dancehall street dance held at 47 Spanish Town Road in Kingston every Wednesday night into Thursday morning since February 2003. There are other similar events variously tagged Early Mondays, Hot Mondays, Blase Blasé, Jiggy Fridays, Weddy Weddy, Blazing Wednesdays and so on, some of which are staged by residents in other inner-city communities. Passa Passa, however, attracts unusual attention because it is held in the volatile area of West Kingston in the vicinity of the inner-city or garrison

community of Tivoli Gardens, known for its die-hard allegiance to the JLP. The assurance of peace and safety at the event is solidified by the fact that Passa Passa is held under the auspices of the ruling , "Duddus", also known as "The President" of Tivoli Gardens, whose sanction underwrites the consensus of peace at the dance.

8. Willie Haggart (William Moore) and Bogle (Gerald Levy) were both prominent members of the popular Black Roses Crew from the inner-city community of Arnett Gardens (otherwise known as Jungle). They became popular as a result of their involvement with dancehall music and culture, particularly in the area of dance, where Bogle stands as the master dancer of merit and fame. They were murdered in 2001 and 2005 respectively.

Bibliography

Abrahams, Tara. "Groovin with the Dancehall Queen". *Skywritings,*
December 1997, 42–44.

Adams, L. Emilie. *Understanding Jamaican Patois: An Introduction to
Afro-Jamaican Grammar.* Kingston: Kingston Publishers, 1991.

Alexander, Jaqui. "The Culture of Race in Middle-Class Kingston, Jamaica".
American Ethnologist 4, no. 3 (1977): 13–36.

———. "Not Just (Any) *Body* Can Be a Citizen: The Politics of Law,
Sexuality and Postcoloniality in Trinidad and Tobago and the Bahamas".
Feminist Review 48 (Autumn 1994): 5–23.

Alleyne, Mervyn, C. *The Construction and Representation of Race and
Ethnicity in the Caribbean.* Kingston: University of the West Indies Press,
2001.

———. *Roots of Jamaican Culture.* London: Pluto, 1988.

Almond, Gabriel, and Sidney Verba, eds. *The Civic Culture Revisited.*
Toronto: Little, Brown, 1980.

Anderson, Benedict. *Imagined Communities: Reflections on the Origin and
Spread of Nationalism.* London: Verso, 1994.

Attali, Jacques. *Noise: The Political Economy of Music.* Minneapolis:
University of Minnesota Press, 1985.

Austerlitz, Paul. *Merengue: Dominican Music and Dominican Identity.*
Philadelphia: Temple University Press, 1997.

Austin, Diane J. "Culture and Ideology in the English-Speaking Caribbean: A
View from Jamaica". *American Ethnologist* 10, no. 2 (1983): 223–40.

———. "History and Symbols in Ideology: A Jamaican Example". *Man* 14
(1979): 447–514.

———. *Urban Life in Kingston, Jamaica: The Culture and Class Ideology of
Two Neighbourhoods.* London: Gordon and Breach Science Publishers,
1984.

Bailey, Wilma, Clement Branche, Gail McGarrity and Sheila Stuart. *Family and the Quality of Gender Relations in the Caribbean.* Kingston: Institute of Social and Economic Research, 1998.

Bakan, Abigail B. *Ideology and Class Conflict in Jamaica: The Politics of Rebellion.* Montreal: McGill–Queen's University Press, 1990.

Barret, Leonard. *The Rastafarians: Sounds of Cultural Dissonance.* Boston: Beacon, 1977.

Barriteau, Eudine. *The Political Economy of Gender in the Twentieth-Century Caribbean.* Basingstoke: Palgrave, 2001.

————. "Postmodernist Feminist Theorizing and Development Policy and Practice in the Anglophone Caribbean: The Barbados Case". In *Feminism/Postmodernism/Development,* edited by Marianne Marchand and Jane Plupart, 142–58. London: Routledge, 1995.

————. "Theorizing Gender Systems and the Project of Modernity in the Twentieth Century Caribbean". *Feminist Review* 59 (Summer 1998): 186–209.

Barrow, Christine. *Family in the Caribbean: Themes and Perspectives.* Kingston: Ian Randle, 1996.

————, ed. *Caribbean Portraits: Essays on Gender Ideologies and Identities.* Kingston: Ian Randle, 1998.

Barrow, Christine, and Rhoda Reddock, eds. *Caribbean Sociology: Introductory Readings.* Kingston: Ian Randle, 2001.

Barrow, Steve, and Peter Dalton. *Reggae: The Rough Guide.* London: Rough Guides, 1997.

Beckford, George. *Persistent Poverty.* Kingston: University of the West Indies Press, 2000.

Beckford, George, and Michael Witter. *Small Garden . . . Bitter Weed.* Morant Bay, Jamaica: Maroon Publishing House, 1980.

Beckles, Hilary. *Centering Woman: Gender Discourses in Caribbean Slave Society.* Kingston: Ian Randle, 1999.

————. "Sex and Gender in the Historiography of Caribbean Slavery". In *Engendering History: Caribbean Women in Historical Perspective,* edited by Bridget Brereton, Barbara Bailey and Verene Shepherd, 125–38. New York: St Martin's Press, 1995.

Bem, Sandra Lipsitz. *The Lenses of Gender.* New Haven: Yale University Press, 1993.

Bhasin, Khamla. *What Is Patriarchy?* New Delhi: Khali Press, 1993.

Bilby, Kenneth. "Caribbean Crucible". In *Repercussions: A Celebration of African-American Music,* edited by G. Haydon and D. Marks, 128–51. London: Century Publishing, 1985.

Bourdieu, Pierre. *The Field of Cultural Production: Essays on Art and Literature.* New York: Columbia University Press, 1993.

———. "What Makes a Social Class? On the Theoretical and Practical Existence of Groups". *Berkeley Journal of Sociology* 32 (1987): 1–18.

Boxill, Ian. "The Two Faces of Caribbean Music". *Social and Economic Studies* 43, no. 2 (1994): 494–503.

Boyd, Derick. *Economic Management, Income Distribution, and Poverty in Jamaica.* New York: Praeger, 1988.

Bradley, Lloyd. *Bass Culture: When Reggae Was King.* London: Viking, 2000.

Brathwaite, Edward. *The Development of Creole Society in Jamaica 1770–1820.* Oxford: Clarendon Press, 1971.

———. *The Folk Culture of the Slaves in Jamaica.* London: New Beacon Books, 1981.

———. *History of the Voice: The Development of Nation Language in Anglophone Caribbean Poetry.* London: New Beacon Books, 1984.

Brereton, Bridget, Verene Shepherd and Barbara Bailey, eds. *Engendering History: Caribbean Women in Historical Perspective.* Kingston: Ian Randle, 1995.

Brodber, Erna. "Black Consciousness and Popular Music in Jamaica in the 1960s and 1970s". *Caribbean Quarterly* 31, no. 2 (1985): 53–66.

———. "Socio-Cultural Change in Jamaica". In *Jamaica Independence,* edited by Rex Nettleford, 54–74. Kingston: Heinemann Caribbean, 1989.

Brown, Aggrey. *Color, Class and Politics in Jamaica.* New Brunswick, NJ: Transaction Books, 1979.

Brown, Jarrett. "Masculinity and Dancehall". *Caribbean Quarterly* 45, no. 1 (March 1999): 1–16.

Campbell, Horace. *Rasta and Resistance: From Marcus Garvey to Walter Rodney.* Trenton, NJ: Africa World Press, 1987.

Carty, Hilary S. *Folk Dances of Jamaica: An Insight.* London: Dance Books, 1988.

Cassidy, Frederick G. *Jamaica Talk: Three Hundred Years of the English Language in Jamaica.* London: Macmillan, 1961.

Chang, Kevin O'Brien, and Wayne Chen. *Reggae Routes: The Story of Jamaican Music.* Kingston: Ian Randle, 1998.

Charles, Christopher. "Garrison Communities as Counter Societies: The Case of the 1998 Zeeks' Riot in Jamaica". *Ideaz* 1 (2002): 29–43.

———. "Skin Bleaching, Self-Hate and Black Identity in Jamaica". *Journal of Black Studies* 33 (2003): 711–28.

Charles, Pearnel. *Detained*. 2nd ed. Kingston: Kingston Publishers, 1977.

Chevannes, Barry. *Learning to Be a Man: Culture, Socialization and Gender Identity in Five Caribbean Communities*. Kingston: University of the West Indies Press, 2001.

———. *What We Sow and What We Reap: Problems in the Cultivation of Male Identity in Jamaica*. Grace, Kennedy Lecture Series. Kingston: Grace, Kennedy Foundation, 1999.

Chude-Sokei, Louis. "Postnationalist Geographies: Rasta, Ragga, and Reinventing Africa". In *Reggae, Rasta, Revolution: Jamaican Music from Ska to Dub*, edited by Chris Potash, 215–27. New York: Schirmer Books, 1997.

Clarke, Peter B. *Black Paradise: The Rastafarian Movement*. Wellingborough: Awuarian Press, 1986.

Clarke, Sebastian. *Jah Music: The Evolution of Popular Jamaican Song*. London: Heinemann Educational Books, 1980.

Clatterbaugh, Kenneth. *Contemporary Perspectives on Masculinity*. 2nd ed. Boulder: Westview, 1997.

Collins, Patricia Hill. *Black Feminist Thought*. New York: Routledge, 1991.

Connell, R.W. *Gender and Power: Society, the Person and Sexual Politics*. Cambridge: Polity Press, 1987.

———. *Masculinities*. Berkeley: University of California Press, 1995.

Cooper, Carolyn. "Erotic Play in the Dance Hall". Parts 1 and 2. *Jamaica Journal* 22, no. 4 (1989): 12–31, and 23, no. 1 (1990): 44–51.

———. "Lyrical Gun: Metaphor and Role Play in Jamaican Dancehall Culture". *Massachusetts Review* 35, nos. 3–4 (Autumn 1994): 429–47.

———. *Noises in the Blood: Orality, Gender, and the "vulgar" Body of Jamaican Popular Culture*. London, Macmillan, 1993.

———. "Punany Power". *Black Media Journal* 2 (2000): 50–52.

———. *Sound Clash: Jamaican Dancehall Culture at Large*. New York: Palgrave Macmillan, 2004.

Cosgrove, Stuart. "Slack-Talk and Uptight: On the Feud That Is Rocking Reggae". *New Statesman*, 28 July 1989.

Curtin, Phillip. *Two Jamaicas: The Role of Ideas in a Tropical Colony 1830–1865*. West Hanover, Mass.: Atheneum Press, 1955.

Daniel, Yvonne. *Rumba: Dance and Social Change in Contemporary Cuba.* Bloomington: Indiana University Press, 1995.

Davis, Stephen, and Peter Simon. *Reggae Bloodlines: In Search of the Music and Culture of Jamaica.* New York: Da Capo, 1992.

———. *Reggae International.* New York: Rogner and Berhnard, 1982.

Devonish, Hubert. *Language and Liberation: Creole Language Politics in the Caribbean.* London: Karia Press, 1986.

Dunn, Hopeton S., ed. *Globalization, Communications and Caribbean Identity.* Kingston: Ian Randle, 1995.

Emmanuel, Patrick, A.M. *Elections and Party Systems in the Commonwealth Caribbean: 1944–1991.* St Michael, Barbados: Caribbean Development Research Services, 1992.

Fanon, Frantz. *Black Skin, White Masks.* London: Pluto, 1986.

———. *The Wretched of the Earth.* Harmondsworth: Penguin, 1967.

Figueroa, Mark, and Amanda Sives. "Homogeneous Voting, Electoral Manipulation and the 'Garrison' Process in Post-Independence Jamaica". *Journal of Commonwealth and Comparative Politics* 40 (2002).

Fiske, John. *Understanding Popular Culture.* Boston: Unwin Hyman, 1989.

Forbes, John D. *Jamaica: Managing Political and Economic Change.* Washington, DC: American Enterprise Institute for Public Policy Research, 1985.

Foucault, Michel. *Power/Knowledge: Selected Interviews and Other Writings.* New York: Pantheon Books, 1980.

Francis-Jackson, Chester. *The Official Dancehall Dictionary: A Guide to Jamaican Dialect and Dancehall Slang.* Kingston: Kingston Publishers, 1995.

Frith, Simon. "The Cultural Study of Popular Music". In *Cultural Studies*, edited by L. Grossberg, C. Nelson and P. Treichler, 174–86. New York: Routledge, 1992.

Geertz, Clifford. *The Interpretation of Cultures: Selected Essays.* New York: Basic Books, 1973.

Gilroy, Paul. *The Black Atlantic: Modernity and Double Consciousness.* Cambridge: Harvard University Press, 1993.

———. *There Ain't No Black in the Union Jack: The Cultural Politics of Race and Nation.* London: Routledge, 1995.

Glissant, Edouard. *Caribbean Discourse: Selected Essays.* Charlottesville: University Press of Virginia, 1989.

Gordon, Derek. *Class, Status and Social Mobility in Jamaica.* Kingston: Institute of Social and Economic Research, 1987.

Gordon, Derek, Patricia Anderson and Don Robotham. "Jamaica: Urbanization during the Years of Crisis". In *The Urban Caribbean: Transition to the New Global Economy,* edited by Alejandro Portes, Carlos Dobre-Cabral and Patricia Landolt, 190–223. Baltimore: Johns Hopkins University Press, 1997.

Grant-Wisdom, Dorith. "Constraints on the Caribbean State: The Global and Policy Contexts". *Twenty-first Century Policy Review* 2, nos. 1–2 (Spring 1994): 151–79.

Gray, Obika. *Radicalism and Social Change in Jamaica 1960–1972.* Knoxville: The University of Tennessee Press, 1991.

Greene, J. Edward, ed. *Race, Class and Gender in the Future of the Caribbean.* Kingston: Institute of Social and Economic Research, 1993.

Guilbault, Jocelyne. *Zouk: World Music in the West Indies.* Chicago: University of Chicago Press, 1993.

Gunst, Laurie. *Born fi' Dead: A Journey Through the Jamaican Posse Underworld.* New York: Henry Holt, 1995.

Gutzmore, Cecil. "Casting the First Stone! Policing of Homo/Sexuality in Jamaican Popular Culture". In "Jamaican Popular Culture", edited by Carolyn Cooper and Alison Donnell. Special issue, *Interventions: International Journal of Postcolonial Studies* 6, no. 1 (April 2004): 118–34.

Habekost, Christian. *Verbal Riddim: The Politics and Aesthetics of African-Caribbean Dub Poetry.* Amsterdam: Rodopi, 1993.

Hall, Ronald. "The Bleaching Syndrome: African American's Response to Cultural Domination Vis-à-Vis Skin Color". *Journal of Black Studies* 26 (1995): 172–84.

Hall, Stuart. "What Is 'Black' in Black Popular Culture?". In *Stuart Hall: Critical Dialogues in Cultural Studies,* edited by David Morley and Kuan-Hsing Chen, 465–75. New York: Routledge, 1996.

———, ed. *Representation: Cultural Representations and Signifying Practices.* London: Sage, 1997.

Harriott, Anthony. *Police and Crime Control in Jamaica: Problems of Reforming Ex-Colonial Constabularies.* Kingston: University of the West Indies Press, 2000.

Harrison, Faye V. "Gangs, Grassroots Politics, and the Crisis of Development

Capitalism in Jamaica". In *Perspectives in US Marxist Anthropology*, edited by David Hakken and Hanna Lessinger, 186–210. Boulder: Westview, 1987.

Hart, Keith. "Informal Income Opportunities and Urban Employment in Ghana". *Journal of Modern African Studies* 11 (1973): 61–89.

Hart, Richard. *Rise and Organise: The Birth of the Workers and National Movements in Jamaica (1936–1939)*. London: Karia Press, 1989.

Headley, Bernard. *The Jamaican Crime Scene: A Perspective*. Mandeville, Jamaica: Eureka Press, 1994

Hebdige, Dick. *Cut n' Mix: Culture, Identity and Caribbean Music*. London: Methuen, 1987.

————. *Reggae, Rastas and Rudies: Style and the Subversion of Form*. Birmingham: University of Birmingham, Centre for Contemporary Cultural Studies, 1981.

————. *Subculture: The Meaning of Style*. London: Meuthen, 1979.

Henke, Holger. "Towards an Ontology of Caribbean Existence". *Social Epistemology* 11, no. 1 (1997): 39–58.

Heron, Taitu. "Political Manipulation and Popular Culture in Jamaica". *Pensamiento Propio* 6, no. 3 (January–April 1998); 243–80.

Hess, Beth B., and Myra Marx, eds. *Analyzing Gender: A Handbook of Social Science Research*. Newbury Park, Calif.: Sage, 1987.

Hope, Donna P. "The British Link-Up Crew: Consumption Masquerading as Masculinity in the Dancehall". *Interventions: International Journal of Postcolonial Studies* 6, no. 1 (April 2004): 101–17.

————. "Inna di Dancehall Dis/Place: Sociocultural Politics of Identity in Jamaica". MPhil thesis, University of the West Indies, 2001.

Hopkins, Patrick D. "Gender Treachery: Homophobia, Masculinity and Threatened Identities". In *Rethinking Masculinity: Philosophical Explorations in Light of Feminism*, edited by Larry May and Robert Strikweda, 111–31. Lanham, Md.: Rowman and Littlefield, 1992.

Horiwitz, M., ed. *Peoples and Cultures of the Caribbean: An Anthropological Reader*. New York: Natural History Press, 1971.

Jahn, Brian, and Tom Weber. *Reggae Island: Jamaican Music in the Digital Age*. Kingston: Kingston Publishers, 1992.

James, C.L.R. *Beyond a Boundary*. Durham: Duke University Press, 1993.

————. *The Future in the Present: Selected Writings*. London: Allison and Busby, 1977.

Jones, Simon. *Black Culture, White Youth: The Reggae Tradition from JA to UK*. London: Macmillan Education, 1988.

Kaski, Tero, and Pekka Vuorinen. *Reggae Inna Dancehall Style*. Helsinki: Black Star, 1984.

Kerr, M. *Personality and Conflict in Jamaica*. London: Wilmer Brothers and Hannam, 1963.

Knight, Franklin W., and Colin A. Palmer. *The Modern Caribbean*. Chapel Hill: University of North Carolina Press, 1989.

Lacey, Terry. *Violence and Politics in Jamaica 1960–1970: Internal Security in a Developing Country*. Manchester: Manchester University Press, 1977.

Lake, Obiagele. *Rastafari Women: Subordination in the Midst of Liberation Theology*. Durham: Carolina Academic Press, 1998.

Larkin, Colin. *The Virgin Encyclopaedia of Reggae*. London: Virgin Books, 1998.

Leaf, Earl. *Isles of Rhythm*. New York: A.S. Barnes, 1948.

Le Franc, Elsie. "Higglering in Jamaica". *Caribbean Review* 17 (Spring 1988): 15–17.

———. "Petty Trading and Labour Mobility: Higglers in the Kingston Metropolitan Area". In *Caribbean Sociology: Introductory Readings*, edited by Christine Barrow and Rhoda Reddock, 801–23. Kingston: Ian Randle, 2001.

———, ed. *Consequences of Structural Adjustment: A Review of the Jamaican Experience*. Kingston: Canoe Press, 1994.

Lent, J.A. *Caribbean Popular Culture*. Bowling Green: Bowling Green State Popular Press, 1990.

Levitt, Kari Polanyi. *The Origins and Consequences of Jamaica's Debt Crisis 1970–1990*. Revised edition. Kingston: Consortium Graduate School of Social Sciences, University of the West Indies, 1991.

Levy, Horace, ed. *They Cry "Respect!": Urban Violence and Poverty in Jamaica*. Kingston: Centre for Population, Community and Social Change, University of the West Indies, 1996.

Lewis, Gordon K. *Main Currents in Caribbean Thought: The Historical Evolution of Caribbean Society in its Ideological Aspects, 1492–1990*. Baltimore: Johns Hopkins University Press, 1983.

Lewis, Linden, ed. *The Culture of Gender and Sexuality in the Caribbean*. Gainesville: University Press of Florida, 2003.

Lindsay, Keisha. "Dance Hall Music: Political Subversion and the Rise of the Ghetto". BA thesis, Amherst College, 1992.

Lipsitz, George. *Time Passages*. Minneapolis: University of Minnesota Press, 1990.

Lovindeer, Lloyd. "Women in Dancehall". *Jamaica Journal* 23, no.1 (February–April 1990).

Lowe, Rich, and Trevor Williams. "King Tubby". *Reggae Directory* 5 (1994): 22–23.

Manley, Michael. *Jamaica: Struggle in the Periphery*. London: Third World Media, 1982.

Manuel, Peter, with Kenneth Bilbey and Michael Largey. *Caribbean Currents: Caribbean Music from Rumba to Reggae*. Philadelphia: Temple University Press, 1995.

Meeks, Brian. *Radical Caribbean: From Black Power to Abu Bakr*. Kingston: University of the West Indies Press, 1996.

Meschino, Patricia. "Who's Afraid of David Kelly?" *Skywritings*, May–June 2000.

Miller, Errol. "Body Image, Physical Beauty and Color among Jamaican Adolescents". In *Caribbean Sociology: Introductory Readings*, edited by Rhoda Reddock and Christine Barrow, 305–19. Princeton: Markus Wiener, 2001.

———. *Marginalization of the Black Male: Insights from the Development of the Teaching Profession*. Kingston: Institute of Social and Economic Research, 1987.

———. *Men at Risk*. Kingston: Jamaica Publishing House, 1991.

Mintz, Sidney W., and Sally Price. *Caribbean Contours*. Baltimore: Johns Hopkins University Press, 1985.

Mohammed, Patricia. "From Laventille to St Ann's: Towards a Caribbean Feminist Philosophy". *Newsletter of the Caribbean Association for Feminist Research and Action* (1990).

———. "Nuancing the Feminist Discourse in the Caribbean". In "New Currents in Caribbean Thought". Special issue, *Social and Economic Studies* 43, no. 3 (1994).

———. "Writing Gender into History: The Negotiation of Gender Relations". In *Engendering History: Caribbean Women in Historical Perspective*, edited by Bridget Brereton, Verene Shepherd and Barbara Bailey, 20–47. Kingston: Ian Randle, 1995.

————, ed. "Rethinking Caribbean Difference". Special issue, *Feminist Review* 59 (Summer 1998).

Morley, David, and Kuan-Hsing Chen, eds. *Stuart Hall: Critical Dialogues in Cultural Studies*. New York: Routledge, 1997.

Morris-Brown, Vivien. *The Jamaica Handbook of Proverbs*. Mandeville: Island Heart Publishers, 1993.

Mulvaney, Rebekah Michele. *Rastafari and Reggae: A Dictionary and Sourcebook*. New York: Greenwood, 1990.

Munroe, Trevor. *Renewing Democracy into the Millennium: The Jamaican Experience in Perspective*. Kingston: University of the West Indies Press, 1999.

National Task Force on Crime. *The Wolfe Report*. Kingston: Jamaica Printing ervices, 1993.

Nettleford, Rex. *Caribbean Cultural Identity: The Case of Jamaica: An Essay on Cultural Dynamics*. Los Angeles: UCLA Latin American Center Publications, 1979.

————. *Identity, Race and Protest in Jamaica*. New York: William Morrow, 1972.

————. *Inward Stretch, Outward Reach: A Voice from the Caribbean*. London: Macmillan, 1993.

————. *Mirror, Mirror: Identity, Race and Protest in Jamaica* (revised with new introduction). Kingston: Kingston Publishers, 1998.

Okihiro, Gary Y. *In Resistance: Studies in African, Caribbean, and Afro-American History*. Amherst: University of Massachusetts Press, 1986.

Owens, J. *Dread: The Rastafarians of Jamaica*. London: Heinemann, 1979.

Page, Kezia. "Dancehall Feminisms: Jamaican Female Deejays and the Politics of the Big Ninja Bike". Paper presented at the conference "Borders, Boundaries and the Global in Caribbean Studies", Bowdoin College, Brunswick, Maine. 11–13 April 2003.

Patterson, Orlando. *The Sociology of Slavery: An Analysis of the Origins, Development and Structure of Negro Slave Society in Jamaica*. London: MacGibbon and Kee, 1967.

Payne, Anthony J. *Politics in Jamaica*. London: C. Hurst, 1988.

Pereira, Joseph. "Africanist Ideology in Jamaican Popular Music". Paper presented at the Conference on the Caribbean Intellectual Traditions, University of the West Indies, Mona, Jamaica, November 1998.

———. "Babylon to Vatican: Religion in the Dance Hall". *Journal of West Indian Literature* 8, no. 1 (October 1998): 31–40.

Phillips, Peter, and Judith Wedderburn. *Crime and Violence: Causes and Solutions*. Department of Government Occasional Papers, no. 2. Kingston: University of the West Indies, 1988.

Planning Institute of Jamaica. *Estimates of Poverty in Jamaica for the Years 1992 and 1993*. Kingston: Planning Institute of Jamaica, 1994.

Portes, Alejandro, Manuel Castells and Lauren A. Benton, eds. *The Informal Economy: Studies in Advanced and Less Developed Countries*. Baltimore: Johns Hopkins University Press, 1989.

Portes, Alejandro, Carlos Dobre-Cabral and Patricia Landolt, eds. *The Urban Caribbean: Transition to the New Global Economy*. Baltimore: Johns Hopkins University Press, 1997

Portes, Alejandro, Jose Itzigsohn and Carlos Dore-Cabral. "Urbanization in the Caribbean Basin: Social Change during the Years of Crisis". *Latin American Research Review* 29, no. 2 (1994): 3–37.

Post, Ken. *Arise Ye Starvelings: The Jamaica Labour Rebellion of 1938 and its Aftermath*. The Hague: Martinus Nihoff, 1978.

———. *Strike the Iron: A Colony at War 1939–45*. The Hague: Martinus Nihoff, 1981.

Potash, Chris, ed. *Reggae, Rasta, Revolution: Jamaican Music from Ska to Dub*. New York: Schirmer Books, 1997.

Price, Charles. "What the Zeeks Uprising Reveals: Development Issues, Moral Economy and the Urban Lumpenproletariat in Jamaica". *Urban Anthropology* 33, no. 1 (Spring 2004): 73–113.

Rapley, John. "Jamaica: Negotiating Law and Order with the Dons". *NACLA Report on the Americas* 37, no. 2 (September–October 2003): 25–29.

Reddock, Rhoda. "Primacy of Gender in Race and Class". In *Race, Class and Gender in the Future of the Caribbean,* edited by J. Edward Greene, 43–73. Kingston: Institute of Social and Economic Research, 1993.

———. *Women, Labour and Politics in Trinidad and Tobago: A History*. London: Zed Books, 1994.

Rose, Tricia. *Black Noise: Rap Music and Black Culture in Contemporary America*. Hanover: Wesleyan University Press, 1994.

Ross, Andrew. *Intellectuals and Popular Culture*. New York: Routledge, 1989.

———. "The Structural Adjustment Blues". Paper presented at the Conference on Caribbean Culture in Honour of Rex Nettleford, University of the West Indies, Mona, Jamaica, 4–6 March 1996.

Saffa, H.I. "Popular Culture, National Identity, and Race in the Caribbean". *New West Indian Guide* 6, no. 3–4 (1987): 115–26.

Saunders, Patricia J. "Is not Everything Good to Eat, Good to Talk: Sexual Economy and Dancehall Music in the Global Marketplace". *Small Axe,* no. 13 (March 2003): 95–115.

Scott, David. "Catching Shirt". *Small Axe,* no. 3 (1998): 115–22.

———. *Refashioning Futures: Criticism After PostColoniality.* Princeton: Princeton University Press, 1999.

———. "Wi a di Govament: An Interview with Anthony B". *Small Axe,* no. 2 (September 1997): 79–101.

Scott, James. *Domination and the Arts of Resistance: Hidden Transcripts.* New Haven: Yale University Press, 1990.

———. *Weapons of the Weak: Everyday Forms of Peasant Resistance.* New Haven: Yale University Press, 1985.

Scott, Joan. *Gender and the Politics of History.* New York: Columbia University Press, 1988.

Sealey, John, and Krister Malm. *Music in the Caribbean.* London: Houghter and Stoughton, 1982.

Senior, Olive. *Working Miracles: Women's Lives in the English-Speaking Caribbean.* Indianapolis: Indiana University Press, 1991.

Skelton, Tracey. " 'I Sing Dirty Reality, I Am Out There for the Ladies', Lady Saw: Women and Jamaican Ragga Music, Resisting Patriarchy". *Phoebe* 7, nos. 1–2 (1995): 86–104.

Smikle, Patrick. "Against Slackness, Lewdness and Gun Lyrics". *Sistren* 16, no. 1–2 (1994).

Smith, M.G. *Culture, Race, and Class in the Commonwealth Caribbean.* Kingston: Department of Extramural Studies, University of the West Indies, 1984.

Sobo, Elisa Janine. *One Blood: The Jamaican Body.* Albany: State University of New York Press, 1993.

Statistical Institute of Jamaica and Planning Institute of Jamaica. *Survey of Living Conditions, July 1989: Jamaica.* Kingston: Statistical Institute of Jamaica, 1989.

Stephens, Evelyne Huber, and John D. Stephens. *Democratic Socialism in*

Jamaica: The Political Movement and Social Transformation in Dependent Capitalism. London: Macmillan, 1986.

Stolzoff, Norman. "Murderation: The Question of Violence in the Sound System Dance". *Social and Economic Studies* 47, no. 1 (March 1998).

————. *Wake the Town and Tell the People: Dancehall Culture in Jamaica.* Durham: Duke University Press, 2000.

Stone, Carl. *Class, Race and Political Behaviour in Urban Jamaica.* Kingston: Institute of Social and Economic Research, 1973.

————. *Class, State, and Democracy in Jamaica.* New York: Praeger, 1986.

————. *Democracy and Clientelism in Jamaica.* New Brunswick, NJ: Transaction Books, 1980.

————. "Values, Norms and Personality Development in Jamaica". Paper presented at the National Consultation on Values and Attitudes, Mona, Jamaica, Institue of Social and Economic Research, 1992.

Stone, Carl, and Aggrey Brown, eds. *Essays on Power and Change in Jamaica.* Kingston: Jamaica Publishing House, 1977.

Tafari, Imani. "Lady Saw . . . Dancehall Donette". *Sistren* 16, no. 1–2 (1994).

————. "Muta and Yasus Defend the Culture". *Sistren* 16, no. 1–2 (1994).

Tanna, Laura. *Jamaican Folk Tales and Oral Histories.* Kingston: Institute of Jamaica Publications, 1984.

Thelwell, Michael. *The Harder They Come.* New York: Grove Press, 1980.

Walker, Melody. "Glamorous, Glitterous: Dancehall Fashion". *Sistren* 16, no. 1–2 (1994).

Waters, Anita. *Race, Class and Political Symbols: Rastafari and Reggae in Jamaican Politics.* New Brunswick, NJ: Transaction Books, 1985.

Watson, Pamela B. *National Industrial Policy: Entertainment (Recorded Music) Industry.* Kingston: Government of Jamaica, 1995.

White, Garth. "Rudie, Oh Rudie". *Caribbean Quarterly* (September 1967): 39–45.

White, Timothy. *Catch a Fire: The Life of Bob Marley.* Revised edition. London: Omnibus Press, 1991.

Whitehead, Stephen, and Frank J. Barrett, eds. *The Masculinities Reader.* Cambridge and Oxford: Polity and Blackwell, 2001.

Whitney, Malika Lee, and Dermott Hussey. *Bob Marley: Reggae King of the World.* Kingston: Kingston Publishers, 1984.

Wilson, Gladstone. "Local Music and Jamaican Politics: The 1972 Elections".

In *Caribbean Popular Culture,* edited by J.A. Lent, 98–105. Bowling Green: Bowling Green State Popular Press, 1990.

———. "Reggae as a Medium of Political Communication". In *Mass Media and the Caribbean,* edited by Stuart H. Surlin and Walter C. Soderlund, 429–49. London: Gordon and Breach, 1990.

Wilson, Peter J. *Crab Antics: The Social Anthropology of English- Speaking Negro Societies of the Caribbean.* New Haven: Yale University Press, 1973.

Wiltshire-Brodber, Rosina. "Gender, Race and Class in the Caribbean". In *Gender in Caribbean Development,* 142–55. St Augustine, Trinidad: Women and Development Studies Project, University of the West Indies, 1988.

Witter, Michael, ed. *Higglering/Sidewalk Vending/Informal Commercial Trading in the Jamaican Economy.* Proceedings of a Symposium. Department of Economics Occasional Paper Series, no. 4. Kingston: University of the West Indies, 1989.

World Bank's Human and Social Development Group, Latin America and the Caribbean Region. *Violence and Urban Poverty in Jamaica: Breaking the Cycle.* Washington, DC: World Bank, 1997.

Newspapers

Jamaica Gleaner
Jamaica Observer
Reggae Connection
HardCopy
Star (Jamaica)
Sunday Herald (Jamaica)
XNews

Discography

BabyCham. "Another Level" (featuring Bounty Killer). *Another Level,* disc 2 of *Wow . . . The Story.* Madhouse/Artists Only! Records, 2000.

———. "Babylon Boy". *The Beginning,* disc 1 of *Wow . . . The Story.* Madhouse/Artists Only! Records, 2000.

———. "Boom/Can I Get A". *The Beginning,* disc 1 of *Wow . . . The Story.* Madhouse/Artists Only! Records, 2000.

Beenie Man. "Matie". *Gold.* Jet Star, 604, 2000.

———. "Slam". *Blessed.* Island Jamaica, 1995.

Bounty Killer. "Anytime". *5th Element.* TVT Records, 6420, 1999.

———. "Can't Believe My Eyes". *Next Millennium.* TVT Records, 6370, 1998.

———. "Lodge". *Roots Reality & Culture.* VP Records, 1341, 1994.

———. "Look". *5th Element.* TVT Records, 6420, 1999.

———. "Warlord Rule the World". Personal collection, *c.*1998.

Buju Banton. "Love Black Woman". Penthouse (Ja.), 1992.

———. "Operation Ardent". *Voice of Jamaica.* Polygram Records, 518013, 1993.

Ce'cile. "Do It to Me". Kings of Kings, 2003.

(Mad) Cobra. "Done Wife". Greensleeves, 1995.

———. "Mate a Rebel". Penthouse Records, 1993.

Elephant Man. "Log On". *Log On.* Greensleeves, 2001.

———. "We Nuh Like Gay/Nuh Like". *Face Off #2.* VP Records, 2108, 1999.

Lady Saw. "What Is Slackness". *Give Me the Reason.* VP Records, 1470, 1996.

Lecturer. "Punany Too Sweet". Jammys, 1987.

Lovindeer, Lloyd. "Light a Candle". *Best of Lovindeer.* The Sound of Jamaica, TSOJ9200, 1993.

Nardo Ranks. "Dem a Bleach". *Taxi,* 1992, and *Strictly the Best Volume 7.* VP Records, 1251, 1992.

Ninja Man. "Border Clash". Jammys, 1989. *Anything Test Dead: Reggae Anthology,* disc 1. VP Records, 1591, 2001.

———. "Murder Dem". Jammys, 1989. *Anything Test Dead: Reggae Anthology,* disc 1. VP Records, 1591, 2001.

Red Dragon/Flourgon and Sanchez. "The Agony/Dungle Lover". Techniques (Ja.), WR24, 1989.

Shabba Ranks. "Caan Dun". *Rough & Ready, Vol. 1.* Sony, 52443, 1992.

———. "Dem Bow". *Caan Dun,* disc 1. VP Records, 1450, 1995.

———. "Love Punaany Bad". *Caan Dun,* disc 1. VP Records, 1450, 1995. Originally released as a single by King Jammys, 1995.

———. "Shine & Criss". Shang Muzik 7". 1993.

Smith, Wayne. "Under Mi Sleng Teng". Jammys, UMST701 7, 1985/Greensleeves GREW091, 1985.

Spragga Benz. "Girls Hoorah". *Jack It Up*. VP Records, 1348, 1994.

———. "Jack It Up". *Jack It Up*. VP Records, 1348, 1994.

Stephens, Tanya. "Yuh Nuh Ready fi Dis Yet". *Too Hype*. V.P. Records, 1997

Supercat. "Don Dada". *Don Dada,* Sony, 1992.

Tiger. "Don Is Don". Personal collection, n.d.

———. "When". Steely & Clevie, 1991.

Yellowman. "Cocky Did a Hurt Mi". *Mr Yellowman*. Henry "Junjo" Lawes/Greensleeves, 1982.

———. "Soldier Take Over". *Crucial Reggae Driven by Sly & Robbie*. Taxi Records/Tanka, 1982.

———. "Wreck a Pum Pum". *Nobody Move, Nobody Get Hurt*. Greensleeves, 1984.

———. "Yellowman Getting Married". *Mr Yellowman*. Henry "Junjo" Lawes/Greensleeves, 1982.

———. *Zungguzungguguzungguzeng*. Henry "Junjo" Lawes/Volcano, 1982.

Videography

Dancehall Queen. Directed by Rick Elgood and Don Letts. Kingston: Island Jamaica Films, Island Digital Media, 1997.

The Harder They Come. Directed by Perry Henzell. Kingston: Island Records, 1973.

Life and Debt. Directed by Stephanie Black. Kingston: Tuff Gong Pictures, 2001.

Ninja Man, Ce'cile and Donna Hope. Interview by Cliff Hughes. *Impact*. CVM Television, 17 August 2003.

Roy Fowl and Donna Hope. Interview by Cliff Hughes. *Impact*. CVM Television, 28 April 2002.

Rude Boy. Directed by Desmond Gumbs. London: Lionsgate, 2003.

Shottas. Directed by Cess Sivera. Kingston: Access Pictures, 2002.

Third World Cop. Directed by Christopher Browne. Kingston: Palm Pictures, 1999.

Willie Haggart's Funeral. Directed by Jack Sowah. Kingston: Jack Sowah Productions, 2001.

Index

Affectees: defining dancehall, xix, 28, 32–35
Affectors: defining dancehall, xix, 28, 29–31
African cultural retentions: vs. European culture, 9
All-rounder deejay: defining the, 32
Anthony B: and the dancehall rasta genre, 14, 32
Anti-homosexual: lyrics, xx, 36, 82. *See also* Homophobia; Male homosexuality
Appearance: and identity, 126–130
Area leader: definition and role of the, 92–93

Baby Cham: and fellatio in dancehall, 52
Babyfather: and masculinity, 52–55
Badman deejays, 31, 86, 87, 90
Beauty: Eurocentric concepts of, 39, 40, 65–67
Beenie Man: all rounder deejay, 32; anti-homosexual lyrics of, 81, 82; "Matie" by, 56
Big man: in dancehall, 35
Big ooman: in dancehall, 34
Biology: gender and, 37
Blackness: and identity, 45
Bleaching: and European concept of beauty, 40

Body: dancehall and the female, 41, 69–72; and identity in dancehall culture, 126–130
Bogle: and dance in dancehall, 30
"Border Clash" (1990): Sting, 112–118
Bounty Killa: anti-homosexual lyrics of, 81, 82
Bowing: in dancehall music, 51–53
Browning: and perceptions of beauty, 40
"Browning": by Buju Banton, 43–44
Buff Bay competition: and erotic display, 70–71
Buju Banton: anti-homosexual lyrics of, 81, 82; colour in lyrics of, 43–44

"Caan Dun": punaany lyrics by Shabba Ranks, 49
Cable television: and dancehall music, 16, 127–128
Cactus Nightclub: dancehall contests, 70–71
Capleton: anti-homosexual lyrics of, 81, 82; and the dancehall rasta genre, 14, 32
Carlene: dancehall queen, xx, 65–67
Ce'cile: and cunnilingus in dancehall music, 52; "Do It to Me Baby" by, 51

"Champion jockey": sexual
conquest and the, 53–55

Charles, Christopher: and garrisons,
92; and shottas, 94; and skin
bleaching, 44

Chevannes, Barry: on male
socialization, 83, 90

Chi-chi man genre: in dancehall
music, 79–85

Christianity: anti-homosexuality and
fundamentalist, 81, 82

Clash: deejays and the lyrical, xx;
between Ninjaman and Josey
Wales, 108,

Class: and acceptance of dancehall
queen Carlene, 66–67

Class structure: and colour, 43–45;
in Jamaica, 6–7

Cobra: "Mate ah Rebel" by, 56

Colour: and class, 43–45, 68; and
identity in dancehall, 43–45; and
perceptions of beauty, 40, 65–67

Contests: in dancehall culture,
69–75

Cooper, Carolyn: on dancehall
culture, 19

Cost of living: 1980–1990, 5

Creolization: and the dichotomy in
Jamaican culture, 9

Crime and violence: in Jamaica,
87–88

Culture: tensions in Jamaican, 9

Dads: in dancehall, 35

Dance contests: in dancehall culture,
69–70, 73–75

Dancehall: defining, 26–28; foreign
exchange earnings from, 22; social
mobility and, 23–24

Dancehall culture: identity and,
xviii; linkages in, 20; negative
perception of, 18; and small-scale
entrepreneurship, 16–17,
123–125; visibility of, 18

Dancehall queen: contest, 65; female
empowerment as, 62–72

Dancehall rasta deejays, 14, 32,
117

Deejays: types of, 31-32

"Dem a Bleach": by Nardo Ranks,
44

"Dem Bow": Shabba Ranks 51–52

Democratic socialism: Manley and, 2

Dis/place: defining, xx, 26–28;
symbols in dancehall, 20

Dynamic hype creators: in dancehall,
29–30

Domestic violence: and poverty, 88

Domestic work: and gender, 46

Don: definition and the role of the
community, xx, 91–93, 98

Don Shotta: in dancehall, 34

Don Youth: in dancehall, 34

Dress: in dancehall culture, 33

Economic crisis: of the 1970s, 2;
1980s, 4

Economic mobility: and gender,
45–48; dancehall and female,
69–79

Electronic media: and the
development of dancehall, 15–16,
127–128

Elephant Man: anti-homosexual
lyrics of, 81, 82; and dancehall,
11, 32

Empowerment: male sexuality and,
52–55

Entrepreneurship: dancehall and small scale, 16–17, 123–125
Erotic display: in dancehall, xix, 33, 69–79
European culture: vs. African cultural retentions, 9

Fada: in dancehall, 35
Fellatio: in dancehall music, 51–52
Female body: dancehall and the, 41, 69–72; and identity, 125–130
Female deejays: rise of, 77–79
Female rivalry: in dancehall culture, 55–62
Female sexuality: in dancehall culture, xix, 48–52, 69; Madonna/whore syndrome and perceptions of, 39–40
Femininity: Carlene as symbol of dancehall, 69; and European concept of beauty, 40
Foreign aid. *See* International aid
Foreign exchange: earnings from dancehall, 22
Foster, Winston. *See* Yellowman
Fraser, Junior "Heavy D": and Sting, 110
Freaky hype type: in dancehall, 34–35
Funerals: performance and, 128

Gang warfare: inner city, 93–97
Garrison: defining a, 3
Gender: in dancehall culture, xx; defining, 36–37; and occupations, 45–48; and sexuality, 36–37, 79
Gender relations: in dancehall, 19–20; sexual behaviour and, 52–62

Gender stratification: in Jamaica, 37
Gendered identity: in dancehall culture, xix, 79–85
Ghetto slam: and female sexual stereotypes, 40
Girls dem deejays, 31
Gordon, Rexton. *See* Shabba Ranks
Grammy for Best Reggae Album, 22
Gun: as a symbol of power, 86, 93; young male identity, 90, 93–97
Gutzmore, Cecil: and anti-homosexual lyrics, 80

Haggart, Willie, 128, 145n8
Harder They Come, The: violence in, 91
Heavy man: in dancehall, 35
Hewitt, Christine, 65
Higglers: economic growth of, 8; stereotype, 46. *See also* Informal commercial importers
"Hollywoodization": of Jamaican popular culture, 86
Homophobia: in dancehall culture, xx, 36
Homosexuality: in the international media, 82. *See also* Male homosexuality
Horseman: dancehall photographer, 30
HYPE TV: and growth of dancehall music, 16

ICIs. *See* Informal commercial importers
Identity: and appearance, 126–130; blackness and, 45; colour and, 43–45; dancehall culture and, xviii, 27–28; 33–35; gendered,

79–85; and reinforcement of masculine, 79–85; gun and young male, 90, 93–97; negotiation in dancehall, 21–23; and sexuality, 38

"Identity and Conduct in Dancehall Culture": UWI Faculty of Social Sciences course in, 125

Ideology: PNP's leftist, 1–2

Independent ooman: in dancehall, xix, 34, 58–59; and gendered identity, 85

Informal commercial importers (ICIs): development of, 8

Informal economy: dancehall and the, 10–12; growth of the, 6, 7–9 and influence of the community Don, 93

International aid: from the USA (1980s), 3–4

International Monetary Fund (IMF): 1976 standby agreement, 2; 1980 agreement, 3–4

IRIE FM: and popular music, 15–16

Jamaica Federation of Lesbians, All-Sexuals and Gays (JFLAG): and homosexuality in Jamaica, 82

Jamaica Labour Party (JLP): and Jamaica's political development, 1–2

Josey Wales: badman deejay, 31; and violence in dancehall music, 86

King Stitt: and the development of deejaying, 10

Kingston: crime rates in, 87–88

Kingston Metropolitan Area (KMA): population, 4–5

Labour riots (1938): and violence, 87

Lady G: and music production, 77

Lady Saw, xx, 62, 63, 65–67; and music production, 77; slackness deejay, 31, 67–68

Laing, Isaiah: and Sting, 110

Lecturer: punaany lyrics by, 49

Lee, Sandra: dancehall queen, 63–64

Lesbianism: attitudes to, 83

"Lodge": lyrical violence in, 90

"Love Punaany Bad": by Shabba Ranks, 48–49

Lyrical clash. *See* Clash

Lyrical violence: in dancehall music, 88

Madonna/whore syndrome: and perceptions of female sexuality, 39–40, 55–62

Male conquerer/courtier: and punaany, 48–52

Male dominance: in dancehall culture, 52–62; in Jamaican society, 37; and masculine identity, 79–85

Male/female relationships: in dancehall culture, 52–62

Male homosexuals: dancehall renunciation of, xx, 79–85

Male prostitution, 46

Male sexuality: and empowerment, 52–55; trade of, 46

Manley, Michael: and democratic socialism, 2

Marley, Bob: conscious lyrics of, 13

Masculine gaze: erotic display and the, 75–76

Masculinity: dancehall and the

reinforcement of, 79–85; and sexuality, 47

"Matie": by Beenie Man, 56; in dancehall culture, xix, 55–60; and gendered identity, 85

"Mate ah Rebel": by Cobra, 56

McDowell, DiMario: and Sting, 110

Middle-class: perception of dancehall, 18–19

Minimum wage: 1980s, 5

Miss Buff Bay contest: erotic display in, 70–71

Miss Dancehall contest: and erotic display, 69–70

Miss Hotty Hotty 32–33

Miss Thing, 33

Miss Vogue, 33

Morant Bay Rebellion: and violence, 87

Nardo Ranks: bleaching in lyrics of, 44

Ninjaman: badman deejay, 31; and violence in dancehall music, 86, 99, 100, 107–108

Noise Abatement Act (1997): and dancehall music, 120

Occupations: gender and, 45–48

Outrage: campaign against anti-homosexual lyrics, 82

Passa passa: and performance in dancehall, 128

Patriarchy: gender and, 37; and male homosexuality, xx, 83–85. *See also* Male dominance

People's National Party (PNP): and Jamaica's political development, 1–2

Performance: and identity, 126–130

Plantation slavery: perceptions of sexuality in, 38

Police: and dancehall events, 120

Political ideology. *See* Ideology

Politics: and violence, 92

Politics of subversion: slackness in dancehall as, 19

Popular culture: development of, 9–10; violence in, 85–121

Portmore: growth of, 4

Poverty: and body image, 41; levels (1980s), 5; and partisan politics, 3; and violence, 88, 94–97

Power: and economic status, 48

Producers: in dancehall, 29

Promoters: in dancehall, 29

Punaany: defining, 48–49, in dancehall, xix

Punaany lyrics, 48–52

"Punaany too Sweet": by Lecturer, 49

Race: and sexuality, 37–38; and status, 7

Race-gender continuum, 39

Radio: and development of dancehall, 15–16

Rasta deejay, 32

Rastafari: and reggae, 12, 13, 14

Red Dragon: punaany lyrics by, 49

Reggae Entertainment TV. *See* RETV

Reggae music: and social commentary, 13, 14, 21

Reggae Sumfest, 20; Dancehall Night, 102–103

Reggae Sunsplash, x, 20, 50, 102–109, 111, 112, 114, 117

Resistance: violence and political, 87
RETV: and growth of dancehall music, 16
Rude bwoy phenomenon: in dancehall, 90–91, 97, 98

Sam Sharpe rebellion: and violence, 87
Seaga, Edward: and JLP's 1980 electoral victory, 2; and leadership of the JLP, 98
Self re-presentation: and identity, 126–130
Sexual lyrics, Lady Saw's, 67–68
Sexual stereotypes: in plantation slavery, 38–39
Sexuality: gender and, xx, 37–38; and identity, xix, 38; and masculinity, 47. *See also* Female sexuality; Male sexuality
Shabba Ranks: and bowing, 51; clash with Ninjaman at Sting 1990, 118; and dancehall, 11, 31; punaany lyrics by, 48–49, 50; violence in lyrics by, 90
"Shine and Kris": lyrical violence in, 90
Shotta: defining the, xx, 94–97
Singers: and dancehall, 12
Sizzla: Rastafari deejay, 14, 32
Skatalites: and Sting (1990), 112
Skettel: in dancehall culture, xix, 60–62; and gendered identity, 85
Skin bleaching. *See* Bleaching
Skin out: and erotic display in dancehall, 33, 70
Slackness: in dancehall, 11, 19, 67–68
"Slackness": by Lady Saw, 67–68

Slackness deejay, 31
Slavery. *See* Plantation slavery
Sleng Teng rhythm: creation of the, 14
Social mobility: and bleaching, 42, 42; dancehall and female, 74; occupations and, 45–48
Social status: dancehall and, 123–125, 128–130
Society: male dominance in Jamaican, 37
Song creators: in dancehall, 29
Sound systems: and the development of dancehall, 14–15
Sound system operators: in dancehall, 29
Sowah, Jack: and dissemination of dancehall culture, 30, 73
Spragga Benz: "Jack It Up" by, 49; "Matie Free Paper Bun" by, 57; punaany lyrics by, 49
Status groupings: in Jamaica, 6; and wealth, 23–24
Stephens, Tanya: dancehall queen, 62; and male sexuality, 51
Stewart, Dr Kingsley: study of dancehall culture, 125
Sting: and promotion of dancehall music 20, 109–118
Structural adjustment: and the economy, 2, 4–5; and changing relationships between political leaders and Dons, 93
Super Cat: badman deejay, 31; clash with Ninjaman at Sting 1991, 118; and violence in dancehall music, 86
Supreme Productions: and Sting, 110

Television: liberalization of Jamaican, 16

Third World Cop: and inner city violence, 93–94

Tiger: and violence in dancehall music, 98

TOK: anti-homosexual lyrics of, 81, 82

Treasure Chest competition: Cactus Nightclub, 71

Two-party system: Jamaica's, 3–4

United States of America: economic aid to Jamaica (1980s), 3

Urban poverty: and violence, 88

U-Roy: and development of deejaying, 10–11

Video: and exposure in dancehall, 64

Violence: in dancehall music, 86–121; defining, 87; and poverty, 88, 94–97. *See also* Lyrical violence

Violent crimes: in Jamaica (1974–1976), 87–88

Visibility: and performance in dancehall, 125–130

Visual creators: and dissemination of dancehall culture, 30

Vybz Cartel: anti-homosexual lyrics of, 81, 82; clash with Ninjaman at Sting 2004, 118

Wailer, Bunny: and Sting 1991, 114–116

Wealth creation: dancehall and, 123–125

Weight: and female body image in dancehall culture, 41

Wi vs. *dem* dialogue: and dancehall culture, 129–130

"Wife": in dancehall culture, 55–62

Women: dancehall and sexual liberation of, 69–79; in dancehall culture, xix–xx, 32–33, 39–40, 48–49, 55–62; in the informal economy, 8

Yellowman: and the development of dancehall music, 10–12, 31

"Yuh Nuh Ready fi Dis Yet": and male sexuality, 51